Digital Transformation at Scale

PERSPECTIVES

Series editor: Diane Coyle

Digital Transformation at Scale

Why the Strategy Is Delivery

Andrew Greenway
Ben Terrett
Mike Bracken
Tom Loosemore

LONDON PUBLISHING PARTNERSHIP

Published by London Publishing Partnership
www.londonpublishingpartnership.co.uk

Published in association with
Enlightenment Economics
www.enlightenmenteconomics.com

ISBN: 978-1-907994-78-4 (pbk)

A catalogue record for this book is
available from the British Library

This book has been composed in Candara

Copy-edited and typeset by
T&T Productions Ltd, London
www.tandtproductions.com

Contents

CONTENTS

Foreword

'Francis: if plagiarism is the sincerest form of flattery, you should be feeling very flattered.'

This email dropped into my inbox in early 2015. It was from Malcolm Turnbull, Australia's prime minister at the time of writing but then the communications minister. It referred to his recent establishment of the Digital Transformation Office, Australia's equivalent of Britain's Government Digital Service (GDS), and explicitly modelled on what we had created in the UK. This followed President Obama's creation of a US Digital Service, copied from the same template.

In the lead up to the 2010 general election, I was leading the Conservative Party's work in opposition on preparation for government. Britain faced a growing fiscal crisis with a budget deficit of over 11% of GDP. At the same time, the UK had become a byword round the world for costly government IT car crashes. There had to be a better way.

I wanted to ensure that the UK could be the most digital government in the world. That didn't mean that it was enough to be able to download a form from the web, print it, fill it in by hand and return it by post. It meant the state offering services built around the needs of the user. I commissioned Martha Lane Fox to make recommendations on how we should proceed: to make government services that could be done online, be done properly online – digital by default. The rest is history. A single web domain for the British government,

GOV.UK, replaced hundreds of separate websites. Scores of government transactions became digital by default. People who wouldn't have dreamed of working in government signed up for the ride, proud to become public servants. In 2016 the UN ranked the UK first in the world for digital government.

Along the way, we learned about what you need to do to make difficult disruptive change happen in government. Some of it would seem obvious to anyone experienced in turning around businesses that have lost their way. Cumulatively, our efficiency programme saved over £50 billion in five years, mostly from the running costs of government. None of it was easy, and there is much more to do.

I am very proud of what the UK started. I hope this book inspires others to do the same.

Francis Maude
The Rt Hon. the Lord Maude of Horsham
March 2018

Prologue

What you are about to read may strike you as obvious. Governments and big businesses have a habit of confusing complexity with substance. This is especially true when technology is introduced into the conversation. Large organisations have grown used to the idea that their world is uniquely complicated and special. The technology, processes and business models they use match this perception of their reality.

Yet the more layers one adds to an organisation, the shakier it becomes. A lot of big organisations have to work on things that are new or complex, and there is no escaping that. However, often they are doing things that have been attempted many times before. On these occasions, being capable of holding together something very complex can become a hindrance. Some people can hold a crumbling structure together long past its natural life.

We all end up counting the cost of complexity taken too far. This includes the UK government. In September 2011, it scrapped the NHS National Programme for IT. The £12 billion project was the biggest civilian IT project of its kind anywhere ever, for an organisation with the largest workforce in Europe. It's difficult to imagine a much more complex challenge. Most of the money had gone straight down the drain. It was expensive and embarrassing. The failure was both political and technical. Worse, the NHS programme wasn't unusual. The UK's first e-Borders scheme, started in 2003 in order to collect and analyse data on everyone travelling to and from the UK, was cancelled after 11 years and an £830 million investment, leaving behind 'highly manual and inefficient' systems.[1] A government review in September 2010 of the performance of its 14 largest IT suppliers found that none of them were performing to a 'good' or better standard.[2] Rumours of a 'Millionaires Club', admitting contractors who had pocketed seven-figure sums, swirled around the doomed borders programme.

In response to this litany of IT troubles, the UK launched the Government Digital Service in 2011. The GDS was a new institution made responsible for the digital transformation of government, designing public services for the internet era. It snipped £4 billion off the government's technology bill, opened up public sector contracts to thousands of new suppliers, and delivered online services so good that citizens chose to use them over the offline alternatives, without a big marketing campaign. Other countries, and private sector companies too, took note.

Faced with the digital revolution, many people working in large organisations instinctively see its consequences as another layer of complexity. To some of them, digital promises a better fax machine, a quicker horse, a brighter candle. In fact, digital is about applying the culture, practices, business models and technologies of the internet era to respond to people's raised expectations. It is not a new function. It is not even a new way of running the existing functions of an organisation, whether those are IT or communications. It is a new way of running organisations. A successful digital transformation makes it possible not only to deliver products and services that are simpler, cheaper and better, but for the organisation as a whole to operate effectively in the online era. As a GDS veteran wrote, digital institutions are those that are open, responsive and effective, led by people who have at least 'a basic level of digital competence, curiosity and confidence'.[3]

This book is best thought of as a set of guides for how to build a digital institution. It will explain how a growing band of reformers in businesses and governments around the world have helped their organisations pivot to this new way of working, and what lessons others can learn from their experience.

This is not the story of GDS. Hundreds of brilliant people contributed to digitising public institutions in the UK. Many of them didn't work in GDS, or even for the government. Thousands more have contributed to similar efforts in other countries. No book has the space to give them the credit they merit. We haven't named names here (other than in a handful of direct quotations) because that would have meant leaving deserving people out. This book also uses an inclusive 'we' throughout. Sometimes decisions at GDS were made by a leadership team or a product team, sometimes by individuals or by a collective. To those who should get a mention, we can only say sorry. Thank you to everyone who worked to make government simpler, cheaper and faster. You know who you are.

What follows draws on the UK government experience, but it doesn't cover everything that happened there. There are many stories from that time that others can tell better than we can. For example, there is not a lot in this book about how digital teams working in departments and agencies went about transforming several of the country's biggest public services. There is little about the quiet political conversations in the background that kept the wheels turning. There is a whole book to be written about how GDS changed the relationship between the state and its technology suppliers, and brought open standards to the forefront of how officials thought about delivering services.

These topics are very important, and they are mentioned in what follows. However, based on the experience of other countries and companies, they are areas where the best response is often determined by the specific context an organisation is facing. There are many paths to building an internet-ready institution. This book focuses on the actions any organisation contemplating a digital future needs to take. The first steps along the journey tend to be the hardest. The advice in this book should set you up to succeed. What that success looks like is up to you.

The organisations that struggle most with digital transformation are old, large, scared, defensive, encumbered by broken technology, and lack curiosity about what the internet age means for them. They fail their users, be they customers, citizens, employees, shareholders or taxpayers. Many of the examples in this book, given our personal experience, relate to national governments; businesses, charities and other levels of government should draw similar conclusions.

None of what follows should be puzzling, surprising or unexpected. None of the practical steps we advocate are unprecedented or radical. We hope the obviousness of it all might inspire readers to reflect on why their organisation hasn't, won't or can't do these things.

Michael Slaby, the manager who hired full-time digital experts rather than jobbing IT contractors, and then put them at the heart of the team behind Obama's two successful election campaigns, understood the nature of the challenge. Getting this right isn't complicated, he said. It's just hard.[4]

Chapter 1

Why change?

I learned [the civil service] is great at managing things, but not
great at changing things.

— Tony Blair, UK Prime Minister (1997–2007)

After all, things are fine. Not perfect, of course. There's
room for improvement. But you're making steady progress. The word 'digital' appears in your organisation's strategy several times.

Even so, something's not quite right. The organisation
always seems to be in the middle of one exhausting 'change
programme' or another, yet nothing actually seems to change.

And perhaps you've even suffered a cyber attack or major
IT failure. An expensive technology programme or policy
initiative is heading for the rocks, with everyone on board
seemingly powerless to do anything but shake their heads
ruefully. The organisation is sitting on lots of data but can't
do anything useful with it. Your employees are complaining
that it takes their computers 20 minutes to start up in the
morning, like an old car in winter. Your competitors seem
to be pulling away from you. The burning platform that
spurs your workplace into action may not have drawn into
clear view just yet, but as the science fiction writer William
Gibson said, 'the future is already here – it's just not evenly
distributed.'

The prize

In 2011, the UK set up a small team in the centre of government called the Government Digital Service (GDS), with the responsibility for digitally transforming public services.

The UK government was spending at least £16 billion a year on IT. Four-fifths of that money was being paid to just 11 large suppliers.[5] Professor Helen Margetts, Director of the Oxford Internet Institute, told a parliamentary inquiry that 'the concentration of the market in the UK ... with a small number of suppliers getting the bulk of the contracts', was one of the features that contributed to successive governments' poor performance in IT.[6] Central government departments were maintaining over 2,000 separate websites, without a single consistent design element shared between them. Online scammers and tricksters revelled in the confusion, creating sites that looked official enough to con people out of their money.

Few people wanted to do their business with the government online, put off by the poor design and incomprehensible jargon. It was still easier and quicker for them to pick up the phone or post a form. The UK scored 10th place on the United Nations' e-Government ranking[7]; not exactly terrible, but hardly a source of pride for a country that counts the father of the web, Sir Tim Berners-Lee, among its citizens. In the midst of this, the country was emerging from the biggest recession since before World War II,[8] led by its first coalition government in 65 years.

The UK's situation at the time was, and is, fairly typical. The US federal government, for purposes of comparison, invests more than $80 billion a year in IT – a figure exceeding the projected gross domestic product (GDP) of nearly two-thirds of the world's nations.[9] According to the Government Accountability Office, 'these investments frequently fail, incur cost overruns and schedule slippages, or contribute little to mission-related outcomes'. As of May 2015, a quarter of the government's 738 major investments – totalling $8.7 billion – were in need of management attention due to their risk.[10] Big bills aren't common only in government. Gartner estimated worldwide IT spending at a truly eye-watering $3.41 trillion in 2016.[11]

Four years after GDS was set up, the UK government announced that it had saved over £4 billion from its IT bills. A new marketplace to supply digital expertise enabled more than 1,200 small and medium-sized enterprises to provide services to government, half of them for the first time.[12] The single website GOV.UK had become the portal for all citizens and businesses accessing public services online, with hundreds of old government websites shut down. New digital services – such as for paying car tax or registering to vote – had digital take-up rates of over 90%, in a country where over 9 million people still weren't online. The government had won national awards for the quality of its writing and design. Open data was published on nearly 800 government services, handling over 3 billion transactions per year. The UK topped the UN e-Government rankings. In less than a full parliamentary term, the country had gone from also-ran to leading the pack.

The stories of GDS and other governments who have truly embraced digital transformation illustrate the benefits of change. Digital transformation saves money – lots of money. It thaws frozen markets and creates new ones. It brings clarity and beauty to a jumbled mess. It delivers rewards, applause and validation. But far more important than all of those things, it makes things simpler, cheaper and faster for citizens, businesses and users.

For governments, it is a lever to change the relationship between citizen and the state for the better. This is the real prize: a vast improvement in the efficacy of the state and a resultant upsurge in democratic engagement. For businesses, it unlocks that most precious and fragile of commodities – a positive relationship with customers based on trust and reputation.

Outrunning the snail

While that prize sounds appealing, there is always the temptation to say one is too busy. Of course you'll get round to it at some point, but at this very moment, there is no time to focus on digital change. The in-tray is full of urgent crises. You have to place sticking plasters on those first. There will be time to step back later.

This reasoning is powerful, but false. In any big organisation, and certainly any government, there is always an in-tray full of urgent crises. There is never a point where a senior political figure can kick her feet up on the desk and say, 'You know, I've got a pretty clear day. Why don't we finally take a proper look at this?' In the fog of tactical fixes, the accumulated strategic debt from choosing not to change your grand old organisation slowly grows.

There is a lot of hype about how the pace of technological change is leaving businesses and governments behind. It has become received wisdom that the failure of legacy companies to survive the internet era is a result of them not being fast enough in responding to such giddying change. This is generally nonsense. Tom Coates, an internet pioneer who worked at the BBC, called this out in a blogpost written in 2006. Writing of media companies terrified by the hardly novel insight that broadband might end up killing traditional TV, he compares them to being pursued by a giant snail. It's not a fast mover, yet they cannot get away. 'The snail! The snail!' they cry. 'How can we possibly escape?' As Coates points out, 'the problem being that the snail's been moving closer for the last twenty years one way or another and they just weren't paying attention'. Many large organisations have watched the internet approach and refused to adapt. Survival is apparently optional.

Governments are shielded from most of the competitive pressures that are forcing industries like retail, media, banking and insurance to transform themselves or be run over by the snail. However, incompetent administrations lose elections. There comes a point in every government's tenure where the distance between rhetoric and reality becomes too great. This motive force of staying in power provides politicians with a strong incentive to want the system they are piloting to work. Ministers want to feel confident that the levers they pull are connected to something. All too often, they realise too late that they are broken.

Politically neutral government officials lack the same survival imperative. That does not mean that they are therefore naturally attuned to delay politicians. Officials are not the opposite side of the coin from their ministers; they are playing a different game. They are also human beings, and the vast majority clearly want to do a good job. Lots are desperate for change.

Many people are already doing their best in fact, but the system they are in thwarts them. Kevin Kelly, the founding executive editor of *Wired* magazine, once said, 'Institutions will try to preserve the problem to which they are the solution', calling it the Shirky Principle in honour of Clay Shirky, an expert on institutions and how they behave.[13] Bureaucracies will also, as one experienced British official put it, tend to 'resolve ambiguity in favour of continuity'. It is therefore inconceivable to them that anyone could even think about putting them out of business without their say-so. This attitude does not sit comfortably with committing to painful and uncertain change.

In many developing nations, where public institutions are immature or not present, digital companies are stepping in, invited or not. In the Philippines, a country where 44% of the population are active internet users, 94% of those users are signed up to Facebook.[14] Thanks in large part to companies like M-Pesa providing financial services through mobile phones, more than 80% of Kenyan adults have a bank account. The global average is 62%. Communications has long been a piece of national infrastructure, the traditional domain of the state and its officials. This is no longer a given.

It is perhaps too early to say whether the giant snail is coming for better-established public institutions. If it does, those in its path may dive for the armoury of regulations, fines and flaming torches to drive it back. Maybe they'll work. But maybe they won't.

The message for public officials and politicians is clear. If you don't change the relationship between the citizen and the state to fit with the internet age soon, someone else will take over that relationship, and in ways which are not always predictable. In Los Angeles, around 30% of drivers use Waze, a smartphone app that allows road users to share real-time traffic and road information. It provides information on things like traffic accidents or police traps. Because it has become so popular, Waze has now effectively become part of the city's transport infrastructure, with the city administration working directly with the company to alert drivers about potential delays. Perhaps that doesn't sound especially radical – just a good example of public–private data sharing. But Waze is now much more than a transport app. Having become a part of many people's daily lives, the app has unexpectedly morphed into a broader policy tool. After a spate of hit-and-run accidents, LA asked Waze to post a notification on its app whenever a hit-and-run occurred. Drivers were effectively asked to report whether they had seen crimes take place. Not something you might expect from a traffic app.

Whether it is always a good thing that digital companies end up playing this role is far from certain. Such arguments are already firmly on the political agenda. The fallout from London and other cities responding to the corporate behaviour of Uber by suspending its licence to operate is indicative of the debates that will come to dominate political discussion. A private company now owns a growing chunk of the public space for transport around the world. Governments remaining reactive, yet bouncing between short-term fixes, won't deliver good outcomes. At the other end of the spectrum, Tencent/QQ, a Chinese instant messaging service, has been cited by Reporters Without Borders as allowing government authorities to monitor online conversations for keywords or phrases and track participants by their user number.[15] Richard Pope, GDS's first product manager, wrote that 'software is politics now'. It is very hard to imagine this becoming less true.

No innovation until things work

When faced with something scary or unpleasant, human beings are excellent at creating displacement activity. This

7

book, for example, was written entirely in moments where we should have been doing more pressing things.

Organisations are collectively susceptible to this problem. It is especially common in bigger, older institutions, where mundane tasks – getting one's basic data in good shape for sharing, hiring new skills into your workforce – have been put off for so long without ill-effect it has become easy to dismiss them as being optional. As the consequences of not doing them are minor and largely invisible to start with, people generally believe that it will stay that way.

It becomes even easier for a large business or government administration to ignore hard yet necessary tasks if they can find something else that has the characteristics of work, while being much more comfortable to sink time into. Fortunately, the technology hype cycle is ready to provide a stream of distractions. All too often, the word digital is conflated with whatever technology fad has made it into the colour supplements this month. Blockchain. Artificial intelligence. The Internet of Things and connected devices. Robotic Process Automation. The captains of industry, ministers and senior officials who read colour supplements during their brief periods of down time see these exciting things and commission policy papers to unpick their potential effect on the organisations they run. The papers are good. But there is a gap – sometimes a huge gap – between policy or business school smarts and technological literacy. This translates into a gulf between strategy and delivery.

When GDS started in 2011, mobile apps were that day's special on the fad menu. Ministers all wanted their own. Top officials thought they sounded like a great idea. Delighted suppliers queued up to offer their services to government. We'll talk about apps in more detail later. For now, all you need to know is that GDS blocked 99% of requests for them. Government wasn't ready for apps, because the people asking for them didn't really know what they were for. They just sounded good. The blogpost explaining the apps policy, written by Tom Loosemore in 2013, quickly became the digital team's most widely read post.[16]

We have seen too many chief executives and department heads proudly explain their organisation's pioneering work on artificial intelligence, say, while in the same breath conceding their back office systems can't reliably pay employees on time. Or running pilots with connected devices while thousands of their customers still post them cheques. This is not to say that preparing for the future isn't right and good. Responsible leaders need to keep their eyes on the horizon. The successful leaders are those who can do this while remaining mindful their view will be ruined if they step in something disgusting lying on the floor.

What is digital transformation?

At the time of writing, the current Wikipedia definition of digital transformation, which rather oddly comes from a book written in 2004, describes it as 'the change associated with the application of digital technology in all aspects of human society'.[17]

This definition is not wrong, but it is incomplete. The word digital has become a red herring, throwing up images of zeros and ones, of devices, dongles and killer apps. Digital transformation is not all about technology; it is about changing the way you work. This is not easy, and many organisations have learnt that the hard way. According to Forbes, 70% of corporate transformation efforts fail as a result of being 'unfocused, uninspired and unsuccessful'.[18] Failure leaves scars, and dulls the appetite for future change.

The practical steps to creating a digital organisation are not complicated. They are just hard, and often uncomfortable. For very clever people – as senior officials and executives tend to be – being presented with simple but countercultural solutions is almost an affront. Telling them that part of the answer to problems that have confounded them for decades is, for example, to 'use the words normal people would use'[19] is not always welcome.

As part of changing your whole organisation, digital transformation means changing what you deliver. You will think more in terms of services that are ruthlessly focused on what their users need from beginning to end. You will choose to build platforms: component parts of digital services that can be used time and again across different parts of your organisation to cut out unnecessary duplication. To succeed in that, you will also have to fix some of what is broken: the spaghetti of old IT sitting in the heart of processes and services, and fraying data architecture creating confusing duplication.

But the biggest change will be in how you deliver. Working in empowered, multidisciplinary teams. Starting with the needs of users. Publishing your work in the open. Iteratively improving what you do. Testing new services with real people. Using tools of the open internet over expensive proprietary options. Writing clearly for a wide audience. Showing prototypes and working code as a substitute for papers and meetings. Building trust between people in your organisation, and those who it works with. Designing with data. Doing the hard work to make things simple.

Much of what follows in this book will seem simple and obvious. Most of digital transformation *is* simple and obvious.

That does not mean that it is easy. Getting it right means getting stuck into the foundations of the institution; the incentives that shape behaviour, the unspoken rules of the game. That is quite a bit more involved than just building a website.

Before you get to that point, there's a basic question to answer. Where do you start?

SUMMARY

- Digital transformation is about building a new type of organisation around internet-era principles, not adding technical complexity to try and fix analogue organisations.
- It means changing how an organisation runs itself in the background at least as much as changing what its users actually see.
- Being forced into a response to digital disruption is a riskier strategy than anticipating and planning for it.
- Getting it right can deliver efficiency savings and improve services for users.

Chapter 2

Before you begin

B efore you can make a start on creating a digital institution, you need four things.

1. A crisis

If you're reading this, your organisation is probably in the midst of a crisis. Actually, that isn't true. If you're really in the middle of a crisis, the chances are you won't be reading this. You'll be reverting to the patterns of behaviour your organisation or government has followed for decades, because that's what humans do. There won't be time for reading.

So it's more likely that you're just emerging from a crisis. That crisis almost certainly had a technology flavour to it. Maybe your IT has not been able to pay your employees on time, as happened in Canada, where 80,000 officials were paid the incorrect amount thanks to an IBM system failure.[20] Maybe the world has realised you've spent many millions on a new IT system that doesn't appear to work, like the Centre-link debt recovery system in Australia, referred to the government ombudsman after creating what a senior politician described as 'summer from hell for thousands of people who have done absolutely nothing wrong'.[21]

Maybe your flagship policy has hit the rocks, as the UK's Universal Credit did in 2013, forcing the department to write off at least £130 million of IT.[22] Maybe you've been hit by ransomware, as 40 NHS trusts were by the Wannacry attack in May 2017, and been forced to cancel 6,900 appointments.[23] Maybe your biggest new website crashed, like healthcare.gov in the US, forcing the president to attend a White House Rose Garden press conference to apologise.

Maybe people are angry, as they were with British Airways when a new IT system crashed worldwide for the sixth time in a year, causing more than 1,000 flights to be delayed or cancelled.[24] Maybe people are disadvantaged, disenchanted or at personal risk as a result of your organisation's failure, as happened to almost the entire population of Sweden in July 2017 when it emerged that an outsourcing deal between the Swedish Transport Agency and IBM Sweden had led to a data leak affecting almost every citizen, including security and military personnel.[25]

You may be thinking that the tried and tested response to this crisis is inadequate.

It's also likely that this crisis didn't come as much of a shock to you. It didn't surprise you that a lot of money was wasted. It didn't surprise you that, despite the warm words and years of work that went into designing and building that next big thing, the outcome for the people using it turned out to be deeply underwhelming. It didn't surprise you that the organisation was unable to sort out the basics for its own staff.

To transform an organisation, you will often need storm clouds to gather. You need a crisis. In the commercial world, crises tend to focus the mind because they can be genuinely existential. Fail to respond, and all of a sudden your company name is no more than the punchline to a bad joke. Sony's reluctance to develop a competent digital Walkman left space for Apple's iPod. Video rental giant Blockbuster airily dismissed Netflix, then went bankrupt when it couldn't compete. Many companies don't heed the call – often those that have become so big they can't imagine a world without them in it. All too often, the rest of the world has no such difficulties.

Ironically, companies tend to be most at risk when they are enjoying comfortable profitability. At that point, it is harder to see the need for dramatic change; if it ain't broke, don't fix it. Complacency of this kind is only justifiable if your organisation is immune to fundamental changes in technology and society. There are few who can honestly say that now. As disruptors begin eating into profitability, companies find they have reduced room for manoeuvre for making the investments they need to pivot into new markets and digital ways of working. The opportunity has been lost. Talented people have moved elsewhere. Margins get thinner. All a company can do now is cross its fingers and hope the tide turns. Usually, it doesn't.

RETROSPECTIVE: KODAK

Kodak was once the most innovative camera company in the world. The company practically invented digital photography as far back as 1975. Their engineers held the patents. Their early camera prototype took photos of 10,000 pixels – extremely basic in today's smartphone world, but revolutionary for the time. Having created this step change, Kodak then stuffed their new invention in the back of a cupboard. The company's first digital camera didn't reach the market until 20 years later.[26]

While the shift to digital technology and changes in consumer behaviour (photo sharing and printing, principally) were obvious trends to almost everyone in the photography industry, including Kodak, the company was too slow to make its moves. As far as most managers were concerned, Kodak was a film and printing business, and a successful one at that. This mindset stalled progress. More agile competitors got ahead, offering products that were better designed and met user needs in a far neater way than Kodak could achieve. The competition either set trends or followed them far more quickly and effectively than Kodak could.

The company's executives knew these challenges were coming, but they became wedded to 'how things are around here'. As Pete Pachal wrote, Kodak was 'too scared to cannibalize its own business to progress'.[27] Successful digital transformation required taking calculated risks when times were good. Kodak didn't.

As this book was being finished in early 2018, Kodak decided to launch both its own cryptocurrency and a machine that you rent from the company for mining bitcoins. Some technology commentators blasted the idea as a 'scam' and a 'desperate attempt to stay relevant'. Time will tell.

Governments are different. Some people argue, persuasively, that the internet presents a genuinely existential threat to what we traditionally imagine 'the state' to be. The giants of the web are operating like mini-governments in many developing nations, and there is no reason to think their role will diminish.

In most established democracies, government has got very used to simply being there. The political cast changes, but the permanent residents in the house of power remain. So do the rules, norms and incentives that guide their behaviour. The machinery of public life – the departments, ministries and the public servants that staff them – rarely feels the bony hand of mortality on their shoulders. There's a reason that the biggest changes to the fabric of the state take place in wartime. In peacetime, complacency is hard to resist. A trifling thing like the web, the domain of geeks, isn't going to dent that kind of embedded self-confidence.

On the one hand, governments exist in a perpetual state of crisis, but on the other, this rarely escalates into a full-blown, all-or-nothing battle for survival. Like anything stuck on eternal amber alert, this leaves most bureaucracies in a state of constant, reflexive jumpiness. It leads to reliance on instinct and precedent. It also encourages officials to patch things over and move on to the next burning issue, rather than get into the messy and difficult business of fixing the problem. They have no time for that.

The good news is that a crisis is almost always an essential condition for digitally transforming a government, and there's no shortage of them. The challenge is choosing the right crisis.

There are two kinds that work. The better kind is something truly shocking, a failure that presents an irresistible political opportunity. These episodes are so appalling – cockups that hit the tabloids – that they cut through to the popular consciousness. Few voters will know or care about the intricacies of why a technology failure almost brought down a flagship policy, but they'll remember that it did. Few people vote for visibly incompetent governments.

Megaprojects and their eye-popping budget overruns are often a good source of crisis material. Nine out of every ten government projects with an initial budget of at least £1 billion end up spending more than originally planned.[28] As a comparative study by the Institute for Government on large and small projects notes, big projects tend to be inflexible, expensive to finance, encounter lots of opposition, hard to predict and often fail to deliver the transformation they promise.[29] Digital transformation has no magic wand to wave away public complaints or uncertain futures. But it can often miniaturise the budget and increase the organisation's flexibility.

The other form of crisis is the slow, steady drip of accumulated failure. Government is a big place. Taken in isolation, individual missteps can be easily explained away. But if you can join the dots, tell the story and get to the root cause, you have a chance to cut through the noise. All this is harder to do than pointing at one big mistake, yet it can be done.

Let's say you have a crisis on your hands that is too good to waste. The press and public are up in arms. IT has failed again. Enough people have seen first hand that the internet era has opened up other, more promising ways of getting things done. It is easy to think that taking this new path will now be an inevitability. Unfortunately, if it were that easy, more countries would have done this years ago.

To have a fighting chance of changing government, a crisis is not enough. Three more things are critical.

2. A political leader

One of the strange things about governments is how rarely politicians pay attention to their department's mechanics. Some of this is driven by constitutional rules. In many countries, there is a formal split between the political and bureaucratic worlds. The minister will tell the government official what she wants, and the public servant will make that happen in whatever way they believe is most likely to succeed.

To make a start on digital transformation, you need a leader who is prepared to engage across these boundaries. Several politicians have stepped up to this role. In Mexico, President

Peña Nieto set up a unit in his office specifically to lead institutional transformation. Toomas Ilves and Andrus Ansip in
Estonia brought digital transformation to the centre of government operations, conferring global recognition on the
country as a leader in digital without buying or building any
cutting-edge technology. Andres Ibarra, the minister of communications and modernisation in the centre of the Argentine
government, is applying much of the work done by the Buenos
Aires City digital team to the federal level. Scott Brison and Deb
Matthews have been vigorous in their support of digital government in Canada. While he was minister for communications,
Malcolm Turnbull was highly influential in pushing the same
agenda in Australia. In the UK, GDS's success was in no small
part down to the support of Francis Maude.

This style of leadership is not just a requirement for government; corporates need it too. Jim Hackett, the CEO of Ford
appointed in 2017, is not a car guy. *Forbes* described him as 'a
strategist obsessed by so-called design thinking as a blueprint
for doing business'.[30] He wants quickly produced prototypes
that can test design against reality. So do his political peers.

There is an equivalence between public and private sector
roles at all levels. Ministers and CEOs face similar pressures.
Much as businesses have different management committees
and corporate board structures, every country tends to operate its own political hierarchies, with varying arrangements
of executive power and lots of different job titles. The hard
divisions and shades of grey that exist between the political
and civil service worlds also have their subtle differences
from country to country (and indeed, within the same country over time). For the purposes of this book, it is enough to
say that for almost all large organisations – public or private
– there are strategic leaders (who set vision and direction) and

operational leaders (who run things day-to-day). The distance between these two groups is often a good indicator of how urgently a transformation is needed.

In any organisation, the principal sponsor will usually have a number of qualities not necessarily common among politicians. For a start, they will be willing to spend their finite political capital on reforming the organisation itself. This is rare. Most people get into politics or to the top of a company because they have a specific cause they believe in or a vision they want to achieve. The machine that enables them to do that is of relatively little interest, provided that it allows them to achieve their goals. Many ministers and CEOs discover far too late that the levers they are pulling aren't actually connected to anything.

For this reason, the best champions of reform tend to be senior figures in their party or business. They command respect from their peers. In the political world, they will have good, and preferably close relationships with figures at the very highest levels of the government. This generally means they have had a relatively long and successful career, and – not to put too fine a point on it – care less about alienating their colleagues than a newly minted minister might.

For governments, the best articulations of the bureaucracy's flaws tend to come from retired politicians. Nick Clegg, deputy prime minister during GDS's first four years, has spoken of feeling 'squeezed uncomfortably between the wish to react rapidly to reasonable public demands for action and the reality of cumbersome decision-making in government, stuck between the politics of a digital age and the analogue arrangements of Whitehall'.[31] Sadly, by the time the political leaders found time to draw breath, it was too late for them to do much about it.

The ideal sponsor knows that public service reform is no vote winner. However, they also know that if they wish to achieve anything of personal and political value – the reason they got into their impossibly taxing job in the first place – they need to get to grips with means as much as ends. To take the long path of changing government demands someone who understands the high cost of leaving the status quo alone. The most successful champions of digital transformation therefore tend to be ministers who have served in two or more different administrations.

Most will also hold a position that can legitimately exert influence over a wide array of government business. This generally means they will be in a central department, such as the Cabinet Office in the UK or the Treasury Board in Canada. This gives them a fulcrum to interfere in the affairs of other departments – hence their need to be a politically strong figure. There is also an argument to say that the political sponsor should not be too senior. Delivering change in the face of inertia takes a lot of time and energy as well as political capital. Presidents, prime ministers and finance ministers who need to spread their resources and favours over a very wide playing field will struggle.

Finding the right political leader for digital transformation is hard, but essential. Most administrations will have no more than a couple of likely candidates. Some will have none at all. But they are out there. You won't get far without someone like them.

3. A team

Government is a people business. You cannot change a government without changing the people who work in it. In particular, you can't change it without making sure a new group of people can get a hearing within the machine.

To achieve digital transformation of government, you will need to employ types of people the organisation may never have had on its books before. The internet-era digital and technology skills government needs to run basic services don't exist in many areas of public life. At best they are found in small, isolated and disempowered pockets, largely forgotten. Some may be employed by suppliers engaged by a department to cover the gap. More often than not, they aren't yet there on the inside of government, but working actively in the outside, with little financial reward to improve civic democracy and semi-public services. The UK civic technology movement was a rich source of inspiration, and latterly employees, for GDS. MySociety, an organisation that Tom Loosemore and Mike Bracken helped get started with Tom Steinberg, a former number 10 advisor, acted as an umbrella for civic and community websites. MySociety convened this community around two ideas: that they would write in open source code, making their work available for free to anyone who wished to use it, and that every website had to be designed with citizens as the first priority. These would later become guiding principles for GDS.

Other networks also contained the seeds of change that would later come together in the digital team. Through books, articles and quietly insistent lobbying, a group of IT reformers kept up on the sidelines a campaign of effective advocacy for fixing government technology, advising the presumptive government before they took office and pointing out the self-harm government was committing. TeaCamp and UKGovCamp, energetic groups of digital people from within and outside government, exchanged ideas, shared war stories and brought more people into the fold. Without these networks of committed volunteers to draw upon, GDS certainly would not have happened so fast, and may not have happened at all.

Before a country can really begin its journey of digital transformation, it needs to find these groups of engaged people. It needs only a few to begin with, and every country has them. We have met inspirational civic technologists everywhere, from Chile to Libya. An excellent product manager, a handful of top-class developers and designers, and one or two superb user researchers and analysts will get you off to a fine start. Even that is a relatively luxurious position; a functioning delivery team can be as few as three good people. A team working for the Peruvian government began with a handful of staff and still delivered a GOV.UK-style single domain for the entire country in 12 weeks. If that talent pool does not exist in your country, or you are unable to find it, then you have no platform to build on. There's more about teams in chapter 4.

This is harder to do in some places than others, but it is extremely rare that there is nothing at all. People with the right ability and attitude are usually out there somewhere. They're gathering at civic technology or developer meetups, or they're talking on social media. Some are working in other nations, but can be coaxed back by the rare opportunity to deliver something for the public good back home.

4. A mission

'Digital' and 'transformation' are dangerously broad terms. They can kill you before you can get started.

The disadvantage of presenting yourself as the solution to a crisis is the danger of scope creep. If you pull one thread, a hundred things begin to unravel. The interconnected nature of problems in large organisations makes it all too easy for people to put forward objections or delays. 'Of course, you're absolutely right that this state of affairs is completely unacceptable,' they say, 'but once this project is finished in six months we'll be in a much stronger position to get started.' The variant on this tactic is for those people to say, 'Well, if you're going to fix x, then of course you'll need to fix y and z at the same time for it to be really worth doing.' This is not a new problem. 'Pushpin politics' was a phrase used to describe this phenomenon as far back as the 17th century. In the more recent words of one very senior former UK official, this tactic is described as 'collecting rocks'. It can be done forever.

There is only one response to these kinds of objection, and it is an uncomfortable one. You have to ignore it. If you want to deliver change, it is imperative you set a single, clear goal of something you will deliver, preferably by a specific date. In the UK, this was the new GOV.UK website. Getting GOV.UK done on time required the team to ignore many other requests and come up with temporary solutions to deep structural problems, until such time that the organisation was ready to have those arguments. You can't have all the fights, all at once.

The initial goal you set does not have to be the same as your mission. In fact, it is better if it is not. Your ultimate aim may be to save billions, improve public services for their users, and transform government. That is what inspires your political leader and attracts your team. However, your initial goal should stick to something smaller, tangible, realistic, low-risk and strikingly different from what is 'normal for government'. Achieving momentum, however small the beginning, is essential.

This goal should also have support from a wide range of political interests, inside and outside government. Picking a party political battleground is dangerous. If your goal confers credit or blame solely to one political party, a change in administration could hamper any prospect of making digital transformation work for the long term. If you have the right kind of political leader, the chances are good that they will support you on this. The stress-free launch of a successful national website on time and on budget is exactly the kind of pleasant surprise you want to create. Failing on a hopeful promise to fix all the government's IT woes is not. Better services, saving money and making happier users and politicians always meets with approval, regardless of the political orientation.

For GDS, the goals were set by a letter from the government's then digital champion, Martha Lane Fox. Martha had taken a front row seat for the disruptive power of digital as the co-founder of Lastminute.com and board member of Marks & Spencer and Channel 4 as both piloted their way through the shake-up the internet had dealt their industries. Five weeks after taking office, Francis Maude, the Cabinet Office minister, asked Martha to advise the government on how online public services delivery could help to provide better and more efficient services, in parallel with her own passion for getting people online.[32]

Martha's letter was an important moment. It established the mandate for GDS and the mission it would follow; to fix government publishing, then transactional services, before 'going wholesale' and creating parts of services that could be reused thousands of times across the government. It also reconciled two different agendas that needed to be brought into a single digital institution: a group seeking to make savings to the public purse through correcting a broken technology market and turning off bad services, and civic technologists motivated by making life simpler for citizens through the web. For the first time, there was a group with a shared mission to digitise government who had the opportunity and cover to do so.

These four conditions are not an exhaustive list of conditions to give you the best chance of delivering real change. Finding like-minded people in parliament and the press, economic pressures on the government to change tack, and a digitally literate private sector are also a real help. Without these four things in place, however, even getting started with digital transformation is formidably hard. It is better to take the time to ensure these are in place than rush to begin without them.

SUMMARY

- The challenge of digital transformation is to overcome inertia. Crises offer an opportunity to do that.
- Before you start, you need a political leader, excellent people and a clear mission.
- You're better off putting these conditions in place first rather than rushing to begin.
- Combine a highly ambitious, long-term mission with an attainable initial goal to build momentum.

Chapter 3

Where to start

Just start.
— Hillary Hartley, Chief Digital Officer, Government of Ontario

By accident or design, you've arrived at a moment where there is an opportunity to make some changes. There are so many things to fix. Where to begin?

There are three big challenges you face coming into any large organisation about to embark on an overhaul. The first is that some will expect you to start by fixing whatever crisis precipitated your arrival in the first place. While that seems reasonable, the crisis in question is often just a symptom of deeper problems. Solving it might provide some clues for what's to come, but the task is also likely to be a dirty, lengthy and unpleasant process. You might spend all your political capital on the sticking plaster before you get close to the real wound. The GDS took its first steps soon after the NHS Programme for IT, an 11-figure failure, was read its last rites. The nascent digital team didn't even try to get involved, because it would have drowned before having the chance to get started.

The second problem is that your new colleagues will say they have seen it all before. White knights flying the banner of the latest management fad are an occupational hazard for the incumbents of any large organisation. More often than not, these interlopers make lots of noise, embarrass themselves with a weak grip on the organisational 'realities', leave some nice slides, and disappear – and things stay much the same as they were before they turned up. In government, officials learn that ministerial enthusiasms often have a short shelf-life, and wait for the winds of change to blow themselves out. Anybody bearing promises of 'change – for real this time' is likely to be greeted with caution, if not outright cynicism. Change fatigue is a common problem; a sense of exhaustion experienced when an organisation is always transforming but not getting any better. 'Digital transformation? We'll believe it when we see it.'

Your third challenge is the deer-in-the-headlights problem. Having signed up to fix a multitude of problems, new digital institutions often find themselves greeted with a to-do list where everything apparently needs fixing right away. Security holes abound in the technology, contract renewals are arriving or already overdue, good employees are poised to walk out the door. No sooner have you stepped out into the road than several trucks are bearing down on you. Arriving as an outsider, your instincts will be screaming, 'I must pause my plan and get on with these first!' There are some things that probably really do need to be fixed. However, don't forget that many of these issues will have been quietly festering for some time before you turned up, often for several years. Ironically, institutions that are notoriously slow tend to be suckers for false urgency. If the organisation hasn't fallen over yet, there's little chance it's about to right now.

Confronted with a large bundle of big, urgent problems and a sceptical audience, there's a great temptation to become purely reactive. That won't be enough to get you past managing a decline. To get on the front foot, you must begin by setting out how you're going to work.

Design principles

The ten design principles were one of the first things published by the GDS:

1. Start with user needs.
2. Do less.
3. Design with data.
4. Do the hard work to make it simple.
5. Iterate. Then iterate again.
6. This is for everyone.
7. Understand context.
8. Build digital services, not websites.
9. Be consistent, not uniform.
10. Make things open: it makes things better.

Lots of organisations have something like the design principles. Some call them values, or a philosophy. Unfortunately, most are awful things dreamt up in boardrooms or management away days, in isolation from the way work is actually being done by the organisation. The most important quality of the design principles was that the GDS didn't publish or even draft them until we'd done quite a lot of designing. Writing down the principles didn't precede delivery, they were written as a result of delivery. Moreover, they weren't written by the 'leadership'. They were written by a team with lots of actual designers working alongside a wide variety of other experts.

The principles sat behind all the best things the team delivered, and helped the digital team avoid the trap of being drawn into reactive firefighting. They've since been endorsed by the World Bank, and emulated by countries and companies all over the world. Tim O'Reilly, the driving force behind open source movement, described them as the 'most significant piece of user interface guidance since Apple's in the 80s'.[33] We forgot them at our peril.

There are several reasons to publish your design principles. For new digital institutions, the most important is to start capturing a new approach that can work at scale for the whole of a huge, distributed organisation. In the UK government's case, the principles were not written to replace the civil service's own four long-established and admirable values: honesty, integrity, impartiality and objectivity. They were written to do something those values were not designed to do – provide instructions for how to actually deliver things. The original values offered a guide for how officials should provide policy advice to ministers; one of the fundamental tasks of central government. Many public officials aren't in the business of giving advice though; fewer than one in twenty of civil servants are likely to ever meet their political bosses. The rest are on the frontline, delivering public services.

Choosing the word 'design' was important for the GDS. Designing services was something that the UK government hadn't actively done for a long time. They had become passive, outsourced verbs – tasks that government officials paid companies to do on the government's behalf. In the 15 years or so before the creation of the GDS, the UK civil service tended to see its role in terms of activities like 'commissioning' or 'tendering'. The argument for using officials' time in this way was largely explained by taking a particular view of risk. In paying companies to design and deliver public services, governments then passed on the responsibility – and therefore the risk – to them. This is intellectually satisfying, and not necessarily wrong; outsourcing can work well, especially in the business world. For government, however, practice sometimes fails to follow the theory. As the public outcry over the behaviour of outsourcers shows – G4S's provision of London 2012's Olympic security and IBM's spectacular 16,000% overspend on Queensland's health department payroll services,[34] to pick two examples – it doesn't matter if a company contractually carries the can. The fallout still ultimately falls on the ministers. In recent months, the UK's experience with the collapse of outsourcing firm Carillion has put the issue firmly back on the political agenda. Framing the GDS's principles as design-led was partly a statement about public servants; digital transformation meant taking some control and responsibility for delivery back into the organisation.

The design principles themselves had to walk a tightrope. Too radical, and they would be dismissed as unrealisable ideals. Too safe, and the organisation would find itself drawn into the gravitational pull of a much bigger and older institution. The ten GDS principles were selected as behaviours that are standard practice for organisations that have grown up with the principles of an open internet. They weren't standard behaviours for government.

Few officials paid much attention to the GDS design principles when they were published. The first audience for the design principles was those outside government, peering in. The principles provided a clear signal to talented people with digital skills that the new team – and by implication the UK government – was taking this seriously. Being public about a digital team knowingly representing a new way of working doesn't see off all the sceptics. However, it can make some cynical heads begin to give some benefit of their doubt.

A word of warning about principles. Distilling the way you work down into a handful of short statements makes it easier to explain and enthuse about building a digital culture to a large number of people in one go. However, the reality of delivering that kind of culture change in a large organisation is invariably messier than those clean messages. Those involved in drafting them at the outset know that principles have to be tempered with pragmatism. Those who join your organisation later on specifically because they admire the principles will not necessarily have an appreciation for the nuance that lies behind them. Left unchecked, this can lead to a bizarre form of ideological debate, where purist adherence to the rules inscribed on stone tablets is more important than getting the right thing done at the right time. Guard against this, and reward those who break any of your rules rather than do anything obviously unwise.

Starting small

Having told the world how you are going to go about your work, you will be in a stronger position to determine where to begin.

The first challenge for a new digital team is to prove to those watching that it can deliver something that works on the web quicker than the organisation has ever been able to manage before. This can be a relatively low bar, so your true ambition should be to produce something that is not just a little more timely and attractive, but a whole order of magnitude faster, more beautiful and of genuine value to users. The strategy for your first project, like all that follow, should be delivery.

Producing working code must be a far higher priority than writing elegant strategy papers that explain what you're up to, defining your organisational structure or getting your office space right. All these things are important, but secondary to demonstrating things of value to real people outside your organisation. Many other teams in your organisation, be that business or government, will have proved themselves perfectly capable of writing good papers and having exciting ideas. What they haven't done is put working prototype digital services in front of users in a few weeks, tested them, and made them better based on their feedback and other data. If you haven't either, there's not much point in you being there.

When we say quick, we mean quick. Quick in some organisations is a year, say, or 18 months at the outside. A working alpha version of GOV.UK was built in 13 weeks. The UK's e-petitions service went live having been delivered from scratch in 11 weeks to a hard deadline set by parliament. These are government projects, remember. That didn't mean those services were completely finished; all are still being iteratively improved today. All began small, simple, clearly designed and user tested. They started as good enough, rather than perfect, and got better.

Your instinct should be to put your work out in the open while that still feels slightly uncomfortable. This can be hard, especially for those working in governments. Officials often keep things under wraps until they are completely sure nothing can possibly go wrong. So concerned are they that by the time the project does see the light of day, the world has completely moved on. A successful digital team tells users very clearly that what they have created is imperfect, but that with their help it will be made steadily better. The vast majority of people will tolerate a quick, flawed attempt at

33

improvement over no change at all, as long as those flaws are acknowledged and fixed.

There are four questions you should bear in mind when selecting your first project. The first two are about impact, the second two about risk. Your first projects should deliver tangible benefit to users while taking on little or no political risk.

How many people will benefit, and how much?

The goal of your first few projects should be to quickly introduce a small but noticeable improvement in experience for a large number of people. This might mean solving a very simple problem that the existing websites cannot. A classic example is the search query asked millions of times every year: 'when is the next national holiday?' In the UK, there was no easy way to find a clear, obvious answer from the government without trawling through several pages of Google. Fix it once, and fix it well. People notice.

Is this solving a common problem?

You will quickly discover that your organisation is solving the same problem many times over in different places. Ideally, you want to create services that, having met a particular user need effectively, can then be easily lifted and adapted by other teams trying to do something similar.

How institutionally complex is it?

The single factor guaranteed to lengthen how long it takes to get things done is the number of teams involved. This multiplies exponentially when those teams are from different organisations or departments. A good rule of thumb for estimating typical project durations in government is to add six months for every department involved. For your first projects, you want to avoid this tangle at all costs. Pick projects with clear institutional boundaries as much as possible, and ideally start work with projects entirely owned by your organisation.

Is it greenfield or brownfield?

A greenfield service is one built to meet a user need that is new (or at least, newly identified). There is therefore not much to think about in terms of how existing laws, norms, expectations or choices provide a guide or constraint on how the users' needs should be met. Brownfield services, on the other hand, come with differing levels of attached expectations.

Getting involved in existing brownfield services and processes is tempting, especially when they're clearly not working well, and are a source of political heat, public complaint or wasted money. The problem with these opportunities is that they always come with more baggage. Technology choices have been made, behaviours set. This makes everything much heavier work, and slows the pace of delivery down. After a point, there is no avoiding these; to become a digital organisation, you have to fix or close your brownfield services. That doesn't mean you have to begin with them. If possible, start with small services that are completely new (as the early exemplar e-petition service was) or so irretrievably broken that you have a completely blank sheet of paper to work with.

Armed with these four questions, you should be able to filter and prioritise different ideas for projects. If you don't

35

have any ideas, various people in your organisation will be delighted to supply you with some. Be wary of taking those ideas without digging into their motivation; they may have no connection whatsoever to what your organisation's users actually need. The most reliable source of good ideas for new digital services is usually the operational people nearest the public frontline. They will know the kinks and gaps in existing processes, and have already worked out how to route around the dysfunction out of necessity.

As a general rule for digital teams working in government, bear in mind that the quality of ideas diminishes in direct proportion with the distance a person making suggestions has from the users of public services. Some senior policy officials, in particular, have notoriously shaky instincts for what people actually need or do in reality. The exception to this rule is those ministers who are more exposed to the frustrations of dealing with the state via their contact with the public. In the UK, the regular surgeries held by ministers in their constituencies often tells them more about their department's failings than time in the office. Hearing repeated complaints about their own ministry in person from an anguished member of the public helps focus the mind.

Relying on anecdotes for ideas is not enough, of course. Your other source of intelligence should be data. There are various sources worth exploring. The web traffic data from your existing websites is a good place to start, not least to help identify how many of the thousands of web pages maintained by your organisation are visited by almost nobody. Data from call centres is also rich with insight about what your users are failing to find out from your websites. Gathering any unfiltered information you can get on user complaints is extremely powerful too, not least because it ensures that those with access to louder megaphones aren't given a falsely high priority. A digital team may need to get creative about getting hold of such data, because colleagues in other parts of the organisation can be decidedly reticent about handing it over, especially if they haven't acted on it themselves. In the UK, data from the Citizens Advice charity revealed many of the government's operational issues, some of which government officials had simply chosen not to explore.

Digital teams should use their specialist capabilities to build tools that allow them to filter and prioritise good projects. To make headway on the immense task of identifying and filtering the most important needs of a single website for government, the GOV.UK team created a web app tool called the Needotron. The Needotron allowed the team to work out which needs should be in scope, see if any could be merged, and agree which should be prioritised according to how often they were searched for.[35] This helped them to narrow down a longlist of 1,800 possible needs to a prioritised list of 900. A lot of work, yes, but a much better use of time. Although the Needotron was never intended to be anything more than a fairly blunt tool, it helped neatly bring together data analysis with user needs.

Finding the right balance in applying principles to how a digital team works is forever a moving target. Different projects will need different emphasis on either marrying insights in abstract data with insight that comes from speaking to real users or finding the right mix of risk and reward when moving quickly to put working code in front of real people.

Having set out how you are going to work and what you're going to do, you will need to find some people to do it.

SUMMARY

- Design principles based on delivery can codify an approach, attract talented people and demonstrate difference from what has gone before.
- It is better and safer to start with small, new, simple and high-profile projects.
- Avoid being drawn into offering to fix the organisation's biggest problems first.
- Release a working service to your users – internal, external or preferably both – fast, and iteratively improve it.

Chapter 4

The first team

Our way of working is to have a diverse team, where each person
brings to the table a different perspective and a new capacity.

— GOB.PE team, Government of Peru

Government officials often have a dismal reputation. This
is very unfair. Most bureaucracies have a wealth of very
clever, talented, committed people working in them. The way
they are organised, however, tends to deliver far less than the
sum of the parts.

As a tribe, the generalist officials working at the heart of
government institutions tend to be brigaded under the heading 'policy'. Policy polymaths are multidisciplinary individuals.
They write well, feel comfortable with numbers, and are economically and historically literate. The best of them can turn
their hand to almost any problem, and come up with solutions
that work beautifully on the page, or in economic models.
Many large corporations rely on similar strategy brains.

While they are often brilliant people, institutions with
a long-held dependence on these analytically adept generalists are now facing real problems. As the internet era advances, an organising principle based around individuals of
the same kind becomes dangerous. If all the leaders see and
frame problems through the same lens, and call upon multiple generations of similar thinkers from the past to validate

their choices, there's a huge temptation to apply old thinking to new problems. Those who go against the grain find that doing so is a painful (and potentially costly) career decision. They go quiet, or leave.

Fixing this vulnerability is not a question of suddenly expecting generalist officials to become good at everything. The recruitment and promotion paths offered in most large organisations tend to reward people who are very good at certain transferable skills: writing papers, presenting arguments, finding holes in numbers, being clear and eloquent. The people who excel at those inevitably end up with a weaker grounding in other areas. That's no particular failing; nobody can excel at everything for a fully rounded perspective, and they have played the game in front of them very well. It is the organisation – and whoever is responsible for its collective health – that must concern itself with changing the rules of the game.

Creating a workable digital transformation is especially difficult for organisations which have spent years valuing certain qualities over others, thereby incentivising a certain set of skills to prosper and devaluing strength in others. For the UK government, policy and economics have long reigned supreme. This created an institution exceptionally strong in those disciplines, and therefore very good at addressing issues that could be solved using just the two specialisms. For everything that requires a different perspective, such as operations, design and technology, the picture is less rosy. This is not an especially novel observation about the British civil service. The Fulton report, published 50 years ago, came to many of the same conclusions; they have been repeated several times in speeches and articles in the decades since (including by us).[36]

Creating an imbalance of skills and perspectives, unwittingly or not, is not unique to the UK or to governments in general. By making it very difficult for people with different specialist strengths to advance to positions of influence, many organisations end up losing those perspectives altogether as people leave to join companies that value them. Digital transformation is not really about replacing old skills with new; it is about balancing old skills and new, and putting them to work together.

RETROSPECTIVE: ORGAN DONATION

In 2012, the UK government began experimenting with new ways to increase the number of people donating organs after they had died. The Behavioural Insight team, also known as the 'Nudge Unit' – a crack unit of policy experts and economists – believed a likely route to success would be to amend the paper form that people used to apply for a provisional driving licence, adding a call to action that encouraged donations. They were working with operational officials in the DVLA to make this happen, but the logistical difficulties involved in updating paper-based processes were slowing them down. Frustrations bubbled between the policy and operational worlds.

Soon after GOV.UK was launched, a meeting was convened at Number 10. Amending the provisional licence form wasn't just operationally difficult; it didn't actually turn out to be that good an idea. Most provisional licence forms were filled out by prospective new teenage drivers or their parents. Neither group was particularly engaged by reading a sentence at the top of a long form that confronted them with their mortality, however elegant its drafting. The Nudge Unit tested one new version of the sentence on the paper form, and the number of donations went down.

The early pioneers of e-government in the UK had long said that a goal for the new GOV.UK should be to make better use of the 'golden page' – the final page of a transaction. In companies, the golden page had become known as the best point to cross-promote additional or complementary goods. Having experienced the jolt of endorphins that came from buying something, the end of a transaction was the place people were most likely to extend their shopping basket. Organ donation provided an opportunity for GOV.UK to test the application of this pattern for the public good.

Creating multiple versions of a standardised end page was far easier and cheaper than printing thousands of different forms. It was also more straightforward to track completion, i.e. whether or not people had actually signed up to organ donation. Most importantly though, it made testing micro policy interventions at huge scale instantly possible. Why try to increase organ donation using a provisional licence form used by tens of thousands a year when you can change the end pages on a car tax transaction used by 20 million people a year?

Working with the Nudge team, DVLA and the Department for Health, GOV.UK tested eight different versions of calls to action on different end pages. These were based on classic behavioural economic ideas of social norms ('people like you are donating their organs'). Some used pictures. Others drew on the old advertising trick of reciprocity ('you might need these organs one day'). The latter won.

Within a year, a few simple words increased the number of organ donors in the UK by 400,000. The changes had cost almost nothing to design, test, iterate and implement. The whole project was wrapped up within weeks.

The organ donation project was an excellent example of what can be done by effectively combining policy, operations and digital in a single team to tackle a social conundrum. Policy or behavioural economics alone lacked the frontline knowledge to avoid the red herrings, or the levers

> to experiment quickly, with real-time responses. Open-minded, multidisciplinary teams can deliver a lot more than just elegant websites.

The internet era has arguably created some genuinely new roles, or at least redefined existing roles to the extent that they will be taken by different people applying a new attitude. Given the chance, statisticians will say data scientists are just chancers with good PR blagging the same job they've been unfashionably plugging away with for years. That's an argument for another book.

Many of the skills needed for digital transformation are not new. The UK government has achieved some proud moments in design, for example (Henry Beck's famous Underground map and Margaret Calvert and Jock Kinneir's work on road signs in the 1960s[37] were both emulated worldwide), and couldn't have done that without employing people who understood its value. Most countries have only recently learned how to be consistently terrible at IT; governments and public institutions laid most of the foundations for modern computing and the web.

More often than not, governments and large organisations have outsourced the skills that they don't prize as highly to consultancies and suppliers. As unloved specialists bleed out of the organisation (often in the direction of the suppliers), those organisations become progressively less well informed buyers of those specialists' services. Before long, officials with little experience in the specialism they are buying resort to continuing arrangements with suppliers that seemed to work well enough last time, as far as they know. In the meantime, technology and the world it serves have moved on. This is how 10-year, 9-figure IT contracts of doom are born.

Generalist officials and corporate strategists left to their own devices, are genuinely trying to solve problems with the best of intentions, but frequently lack the full set of tools they need to address them. This is where the value of diverse teams comes in. When you're building anything with a national or global reach (and that is at the heart of most digital products or services), your team needs to look like who it's trying to reach.

In the first few years of the GDS, we did not collectively spend enough time working closely with policy experts, getting to grips with all the many intricacies of their role. While many who started their career in 'traditional' roles ended up moving over to the digital fold, not enough made the journey the other way. Building up empathy on both sides is hard work, but is the only way to build a shared understanding in the digital team of the day-to-day frustrations of colleagues who they will later need as allies and peers. One of the biggest irritations faced daily by government officials was the inadequacy of the technology they had to work with, and the block this put on collaborative working; steam-powered laptops, clunky e-mail, old phones, inaccurate staff directories. We didn't prioritise fixing our colleagues' working tools early enough. Had we done so, creating multidisciplinary teams that brought together the various tribes of government could have been done more quickly.

That it took us a long time to begin fixing this problem was a mistake, because a huge part of building a successful digital institution means introducing – or reintroducing – specialist skills into an organisation that has lost them and forgotten how to manage or arrange them. Just bringing in new skills is not enough, however. The real trick is putting those specialists into agile, multidisciplinary teams, working together with various flavours of generalist to a shared goal, service or product. In digital government, the unit of delivery must be the team, not the individual.

Scaling the walls

Putting together an agile team with the right blend of skills is an art, not a science.

Agile teams work in the knowledge that the future is unknowable. The problem that needs to be solved will change over time, and so will the ideal size and composition of the team. There are really only two golden rules for putting together the right group of people. If all the people in that team are good at different things, you're probably on the right lines. If the team is collectively good at solving different types of problem over time, so much the better.

Both of these statements are countercultural to how most governments and large organisations arrange themselves. Organisational design tends to be the output of a powerful blend of inertia, power dynamics, unwritten office politics and leadership behaviour. In general, institutions operating at the scale of government organise themselves into as many silos as possible. The most visible of these are the departments or ministries, where activity is broken down into policy buckets of ever-diminishing size, like Russian dolls. On top of this is an additional layer of arrangement where people with different skills – IT, HR, economics, science, policy, and so on – are clustered together according to what they're good at. A good agile product team must ignore both sets of walls to combine different skills (from different ministries if the product demands it) in a single team and place.

As well as scaling the organisational walls, agile product teams demand a degree of flexibility over time. Again, most big organisations don't cope well with this – a person joins a team to do a particular role, and they keep doing that role until they do something about it themselves, or the organisation goes through some seismic (and often badly handled) reorganisation. This happens in organisations that call people 'resources', because they are filed away, much like staplers and carbon paper. Agile teams that work well move people according to where they're needed to address the highest priority of the time. Sometimes these mini-reorganisations are painful too. The difference is the expectation; people do not join an agile team thinking they will be there to do the same job indefinitely.

You will be told several times that flexible, multidisciplinary teams simply cannot work in your organisation. When you begin on the journey, that is probably true. So one of the first things your new digital institution needs to prove is that you can not only make agile teams work, but that they can deliver things that have eluded equally talented public servants that are organised in the traditional way.

Minimum viable team

Your first digital products will define the trajectory of your digital institution and what it does. Your first digital team will define the working culture and how things are done. There are a handful of hires you need to start with.

Product manager

The product manager is the first among equals in the team, and the public face of the project. They define and articulate the vision for what is being built, explaining that to the team and the wider organisation they operate in. As well as being the voice of their product's users, they must also understand the environment they operate in. They need to be able to judge the right time to come to a compromise, and when to go into battle on the user's behalf. The product manager ultimately prioritises what get built, when. They choose what the team's next hypothesis to test will be.

Delivery manager

The delivery manager is the ying to the product manager's yang. While the product manager tells the world what the team is up to, the delivery manager translates their vision into discrete tasks for the team. They act as the go-between between the product manager's ambitions and the reality of what a team can do. They do what needs to be done to keep the team working in the same direction autonomously. And crucially, they are the fixer. Delivery managers remove blockers to the team getting things done, from finding the right people to fill gaps in the team, to banging any arguing heads together.

Lead developer

The lead developer is the team's engine room. They build software with a focus on what users need from your service and how they'll use it. Their job is to write, adapt, maintain and support code, and solve technical problems. The ideal developers for an agile team working in government are those who care far more deeply about building something that works for users rather than the programming language being used.

They should have an up-to-date knowledge of programming languages, but not be too concerned about using whatever happens to be the bleeding-edge code of the moment.

Designer

The designer ensures that the service presents a clear, consistent experience for whoever uses it. Depending on the project and how mature it is, different design skills come to the fore. For a small team in the early stages of building a new service, an interaction designer who can do a bit of front-end coding is gold dust – they can get you through to the point of producing early prototypes with effective visual cues while you find the right developers for the medium term. As the service touches on more dependencies elsewhere in the organisation, service designers with a view of the bigger picture become ever more valuable.

User researcher

The user researcher is responsible for giving the team reliable, regular feedback from users on their work, and ensuring that the team understands how that feedback translates into changes to whatever they are designing or operating. They will find and recruit research participants, run research sessions (attended by everyone in the team) and interpret the results. User research is not like a typical government consultation exercise. The skilled researcher knows that the real value of user feedback is not in the words they say but the gaps in between. People might say they love your new website, but their stumbling around the page to find the right link tells a different story.

When the GDS began work on the early versions of GOV. UK, we were rightly criticised for having no user researchers in the team from the start.[38] This was a big mistake – one which we went some way towards addressing by hiring the superb user researcher who criticised us in the first place – user researchers are essential members of any good digital service team.

Content designer

We take it for granted that government is a words industry. Thousands of officials do little but write. You would think finding skilled writers inside government should therefore be easy. However, writing for ministers is a very different skill to writing for the web. Five million adults in the UK are functionally illiterate, with a reading age below 11.[39] The content designer is responsible for making the written content on your service tailored to what users need and expect. For mainstream services, that means writing for all. Governments have a penchant for valuing what is clever rather than what is clear. Most users have no need for clever.

Like user research, content design was not given enough emphasis at the very beginning of the GDS. And like user research, it was another exceptional woman who defined the discipline and gave it a rightful place in service teams, literally writing the book on content design.[40]

Depending on the project and the individuals you find, some of these roles can be conflated in the very earliest stages – one person can double up as product and delivery manager, a designer can moonlight as a front-end developer – but not for long. Most of these early hires will be the first people known by their job title in the organisation. They will effectively define what it means to be a 'product manager' or 'content designer'. Over time, these will be the people you will look to lead their profession across the organisation, creating communities of practice and setting the standards for what good looks like.

There are a few more roles you might have expected to see on this list. This is the group of people that get you started, not the entirety of the team. We'll come to other roles later on.

Job titles in the digital job market evolve on an almost daily basis. In the GDS, we used this to our advantage, creating new job titles in order to differentiate more clearly the skills and attitudes we needed in the team. The differences between 'content design' and 'copywriter', or 'engagement' and 'communications', might look very subtle to an non-specialist eye, but that is the point – you don't want to hire a non-specialist who can tick the standard job application boxes.

Most roles as defined by recruiters now come with a certain set of first impressions attached, depending on who is reading the CVs. As someone trying to build the team, you should avoid rejecting applicants with job titles that on first glance don't appear to fit. Sometimes they really won't. Nonetheless, you should dig deep into what the applicants believe they're applying for, their understanding of the skill sets described above, and their experience of working in an environment following agile, open and iterative working patterns.

Finding your team

Recruiting a first team is not easy. Your institution probably hasn't hired people like this before, and you may not be completely confident in what you're looking for yourself. The standard interview and hiring requirements are unhelpful in giving a fair assessment of the type of skills you need. You can't pay market rates. Finally, and most importantly, bringing new staff into large organisations tends to be a drawn-out process, taking months. You don't have months.

Putting the delivery team together is the first real test of a new digital institution. Almost by definition, it is impossible to do by following standard procedures. To make it happen means for the first time people other than you will have to take on some risk. Your prospective new hires must gamble on leaving good jobs for your sketchy but exciting opportunity. For the person who allows you to bend the recruitment rules, they have to spend some of their finite personal capital on something not done before. You need a relationship of trust on both sides of the interview table.

For your new hires, it is much easier to build a relationship of trust if you are not starting from scratch. This is where the power of networks comes in.

In the UK, many of the first hires into government came from groups of people that had been quietly interested in taking on the task for years. By the time the conditions fell into place for creating a digital institution inside the machine, names were already pencilled in against roles on the teamsheet. Some of these people were direct connections, others came highly recommended by trusted friends and former colleagues.

To build your first team, the ideal place to start is plugging in to your network of similarly minded individuals. However, that may not be enough, or you may not have one. In which case, the first step is to find out where those people are currently gathering in your country or industry. They will be out there. Technologist meetups and hackdays – of product managers, or designers, or coders – can be found all over the world. These are rooms full of people who have given up their free time and scarce skills to work on problems you want to fix. It's not a bad place to start.

However, it is important not to forget that there will be exceptional people already in your organisation. Their job titles may not match the ones you're looking for, but the best will adapt to become exemplars of those specialisms. Many of the people who moved mountains in the GDS – often in relatively unsung roles – had been civil servants for a long time, either in GOV.UK's predecessors or other departments. None of them had 'digital' sounding roles, but all proved they had the capability to become extremely able in them.

It is not a question of hiring everyone on the spot. All you need to start with is your initial team, remember. The people you need for that first wave are those who are highly talented, want to be part of your mission and command deep credibility within the networks you are courting. Turning up at a hackathon and saying 'I'm from the government/MegaCorp – come and work with us' will not go down well. Having expert leaders play an ambassadorial role to that world for you, saying 'I'm willing to take a punt on this,' will confer far more credibility.

Exactly the same principle applies to recruiters who help you on the search. The GDS was very lucky to have recruiters who could turn up at technology meetups and fit in. Understanding what would give off the wrong messages at an unconference or hackathon event is not an intuitive skill; every subculture has its own norms, jargon and taboos. To attract digital talent from that world, you need to make the effort to be of it, rather than be seen to be exploiting it.

Tapping into networks like this risks sounding like favouritism. There's some validity to that. Be careful. Only hiring your friends won't help you or them.

With hiring, a digital team will get out what it puts in. The lazier alternatives to finding the right networks are using traditional recruiters or throwing out an advert to the world. Until you've worked with them for a few years, some recruitment agencies will hear the word 'digital' and send you the same pile of IT CVs they've had for years. Not a good use of anyone's time. The public job advert route is perfectly valid and may turn up brilliance. Unfortunately, if your institution has no reputation for hiring the kind of people you're looking for, those people will not be keeping an eye on your adverts. On the happy chance some of them are, it will take anything up to six months to actually get somebody in.

Even by following networks of trust, you won't make the right choices every time. Some of your hires will be the wrong people. We made mistakes. So did some of our hires, who quickly realised that working in government was not for them. Make sure the arrangements you reach make it easy for both sides to shake hands and part ways with the minimum of strife. Then go again.

Bear in mind that bringing in outsiders can create tensions. It is easy to forget that many organisations – and especially governments – tend to offer more flexibility in rewarding outsiders than they do for people that have already put in many years of good work into the institution. Disparities in pay, attitude and behaviour do not guarantee resentment, but neither are they helpful. Be constantly mindful of the need for fairness.

Working patterns

Having brought people into the building, the way your first team works together will impact on everything to come. The traits established by the first 10 or so people in your digital team will end up defining the culture and working practices to come. As much as possible, they should feature some of the following.

Agile

There are as many definitions of agile as there are people who have heard of it. Agile, with a capital A, has become a project management philosophy, with all the artefacts, true believers and factions that come with it. Many of the biggest, loudest red-in-the-face arguments in digital government took place over the one true meaning of agile. It really doesn't matter.

What matters is teams focused on user needs, delivering iteratively in small, incremental improvements, failing fast, constantly planning for the future, and thinking about how to improve how the team itself works together.

Agile working imposes regular working rhythms on a team, designed to keep pace and momentum high: short stand-ups at the start of each day, week- or fortnight-long 'sprints' setting defined priorities and goals, regular retrospectives to reflect on how well the team is working together and allow a chance for people to let off steam. Encountering this for the first time, government officials used to a meeting cycle of monthly four-hour programme boards were either intrigued or dismissive.

And that was part of the point. The UK government had long ago created and owned a project management methodology called PRINCE2, based on an system originally developed for IT projects in 1989. PRINCE stands for PRojects IN Controlled Environments, and when it is applied to controlled environments, the ideas still hold up pretty well. The government was legitimately proud of its step-by-step, methodical framework, but unfortunately also blinded to the limitations of waterfall-style thinking. When rigid structures like PRINCE2 are applied to everything, including the famously uncontrollable combination of human beings and rapidly evolving technology, trouble inevitably ensues.

Working to an agile methodology was a choice taken to define much about what government digital shouldn't be, as much as what it should. It was an explicit rejection of using a model of government project management as a one-size-fits-all answer, loosely summed up by the term 'waterfall'. Although the textbooks and courses tended to offer more nuance, the reality of waterfall-based projects treated building IT systems the same way as building bridges and submarines. Gather a list of requirements first, build, test, launch, done. Waterfall-style methods can work perfectly well in controlled environments. You build a bridge because you want to go from x to y, and you build it from steel and reinforced concrete because they are the best materials. Neither of these things will change that much in 50 years. Waterfall works much less well in a landscape where people's needs and the underlying technology are constantly changing. Agile is a rejection of applying false certainty to delivering policy with technology.

Digital public services are infrastructure, but of a different kind. When they're live, they're just that – live, as ongoing, maintained services. Services whose users will have needs that will change over time. That means teams have to keep updating and iterating them.

As agile has grown in popularity, it has spawned a wide variety of imitators, many of them combining bits of agile and bits of waterfall. 'Wagile' doesn't offer the best of both worlds though; you won't get the thing you planned on the date you planned it, and you won't get something that meets user needs either.[41]

Open

If the idea that bureaucrats can have meetings without chairs is operating at the edges of what is conceivable for some, those same officials actively deciding to talk in public about what they were doing was downright unthinkable.

From the outset, your first team must have a strong bias towards working in the open. Publishing code and design patterns on Github or similar is essential. This will enable teams in different departments and different buildings to follow each other's lead. It encourages collaboration and stops duplication of work.

For communications, it means publishing regular updates on the web, rather than sending round internal memos. Most teams default to emailing updates to a select group of 'stakeholders'; in government, this comprises the usual trade bodies, political figures and media commentators. The well-organised and loud end up getting a disproportionate say over the outcome. Internet-era tools make it easier to communicate with everyone that matters, unfiltered.

Blog posts are good for long-form content, and setting up a blog for the digital institution is a priority. Twitter, Facebook, Instagram and other platforms all have value too. Talking and writing about what the team is doing shouldn't be the responsibility of 'the comms person'. Everyone – developers, designers, managers – is expected to take part. (We talk more about this in chapter 9.) Communicating the project's progress is a part of delivery and helps teams work better. This is not a corporate PR exercise to create a parallel universe where the rhetoric outstrips the reality. People will see through that.

Openness is not just about the platforms used to communicate. What is said on them should be as open as possible
too. Being candid about what didn't work is as important as
celebrating what did. Again, this is unfamiliar and uncomfortable territory for most public institutions. But there is no
question that admitting early to a failed experiment or minor
error shows more humility and builds trust.

Being open as a team is not an easy thing to teach, especially if your staff come from an organisation with a culture
of not saying anything publicly unless absolutely necessary.
Your first team will have people with experience of working
for organisations that are open by default. They already know
it is not as scary as it looks.

Flat

The roles you hire for your first team are far more important
than the structure you put them in. Agile teams are at their
best when they're small, autonomous and self-organising
units, trusted to get on with it. A good product manager will
set the direction and make sure it is in tune with the wider organisation, and a good delivery manager will corral the team
members to run in the same direction. From that point on,
however, the team is a group of peers. The vast majority of
strategic decisions are discussed collectively. Far more often
than not, the role of the product manager in these discussions
is to act as chairperson and referee, not despot.

Putting emphasis on having an egalitarian and democratic working environment might sound suspiciously like a
floaty Silicon Valley ideal. Not everybody is comfortable with
this kind of hierarchical ambiguity. However, adopting a flat
structure is an intensely practical thing to do when it comes

to building digital services. Done properly, it makes decision making and delivery quicker than passing things up and down a chain of command.

Most big organisations, and governments especially, are slowed down by the constant need to escalate decisions and communicate the outcome back down. Senior managers become a bottleneck, progress grinds to a halt. Because a rejected paper will waste even more time, most downtrodden underlings spend most of their time trying to anticipate the whims of their mercurial managers, rather than thinking about what the right answer should really be.

A phrase you hear a lot in big, hierarchical organisations is 'that decision is above my pay grade'. This phrase always gives off a bad smell. Sometimes it is a failure of managers to give their staff backing and autonomy. Sometimes it is junior staff kicking the can down the road because they can. Either way, not taking responsibility makes everything slower.

In your first product team, there are no decisions that are above anyone's pay grade. The vision set by the product manager should empower everyone in the team to make decisions within their field of expertise on their own.

Together

Choosing to set up teams as agile, open and flat is largely about setting the cultural weather of your organisation. Culture is a nebulous thing, hard to put your finger on. You can't see agility. The team's working space is where that culture takes physical shape.

Your first digital product team must work together in the same space, full time. This seems like a ridiculously basic thing to say, but more often than not it just doesn't happen.

The developers are on the third floor, the designers on the fifth and the frontline experts in another city. The managers spend 80% of their time in yet another building. The user researcher is from an agency and only does two days a week. If your team looks like this, you can forget about getting anything done. As much as possible, your team must be physically co-located. No member should have to raise their voice above normal talking volume to get the attention of another. That doesn't mean remote or part-time working is impossible, but it is the responsibility of the team to have a discussion about what working patterns will suit both the product and everyone in the team.

That working space should make it obvious that the default behaviour is openness. You need space to have stand-up meetings, walls to track progress on, desks without barriers between (cubicles are a drain on productivity, and the soul). You need somewhere where people can escape to get on with things in peace now and again. You need some meeting spaces. None of this is hard. Pool tables, martini bars and mini fridges are not required. Things on walls, decent computers and stickers will get you most of the way. The digital revolution can be found in Rymans.[42]

It is important to have an environment that looks visibly different to the rest of the organisation. Again, this should be obvious, not ostentatious. The colourful walls of digital teams – both in the GDS and in departments – intrigued politicians, and made them want to find out what was going on.

Driven

Most of the cultural norms set by your first team will represent conscious, deliberate choices. The behaviours you really need to watch out for are those that are unconscious. If you're not careful, they can become unsustainable.

The very nature of the people attracted to the opportunity of driving a major change in the heart of a big organisation or government is that they are highly motivated and driven. Nobody takes on a job like this for a quiet life.

Running hot early on in a product team's life is often the right thing to do – a new project needs to gain momentum, build up credibility and find supporters. Working hard to begin with pays dividends. The challenge is knowing when to slow down and recuperate for the next challenge.

The first two years of the GDS were intensely productive. They were also exhausting for many people; staff were committed, passionate and determined to seeing changes through – a culture set in train by the very first product team. The physical, mental and technical debt of moving that fast accumulates over time. Burnout becomes a case of when, not if. The ripples from your first team will shape how the organisation keeps the wellbeing of staff at the front of its mind. Heed the warning signs.

Summary

- Multidisciplinary teams, incorporating traditional corporate roles and digital skills, are essential for successful digital institutions.
- The unit of delivery is the team.
- All team practices should have a strong bias towards open, agile, flat and co-located working.
- Find the right people; don't expect them to find you. Look to trusted networks and expert communities.

Chapter 5

Preparing the ground

After they join together, a new digital team should spend a few months operating under the radar, getting on with building things. Politicians and senior executives alike can be tempted to launch their new initiatives with great fanfare before they have anything of substance to show. A new digital institution should avoid this at all costs. The time to break cover is after you have shipped something. You must be able to show, not just tell.

The other advantage to holding back on a big launch is that it gives a team more time to prepare for the increased exposure that going public will bring – both within the organisation and to the outside world. Each step a digital team takes towards gaining more visibility increases its influence, while sharpening the risk of damage if something going wrong. You need to be ready for the power and responsibility. It is good for the stakes to increase, but steadily.

No matter how good your delivery team is, the people in this small group are not who should be worrying about the organisation's future. Their focus must remain on shipping early versions of products and services that meet user needs, and making sure they get better as a delivery team. To do that, they will need cover from the paperwork, plaudits and protestations that could slow them down.

In governments and companies operating on a large scale, there are three layers of people that are essential in protecting the quality and pace of delivery.

Political cover

Ministers decide. That is the crux of their job. They may spend plenty of time on other things; as parliamentarians, constituency cheerleaders, and (in some cases) broadcasters across the nation's media. Their time on the government payroll, however, is mostly spent selecting a preferred option from the steady parade of menus put in front of them by their advisers and officials. Having extricated themselves from this treadmill, some ex-ministers belatedly realise that they didn't have time to do a scrap of original thinking themselves.

Inertia is the most powerful force in government. Left alone without political direction, government departments don't stop doing things. By default, they maintain whatever holding pattern was left behind by the previous occupant of the minister's chair. If there is no active political hand on the tiller for a long period of time, officials simply get on with preparing an unending pile of options papers, in anticipation of every possible question they could face in the event of a minister who is not lazy or distracted turning up. *

The biggest card a minister seeking to influence society can play is to overcome that inertia, and change the momentum behind a particular issue. In the minister's view, the bureaucracy's unchecked efforts might be moving too slowly in the right direction, have ground to a complete halt or be heading down the wrong path.

In theory, new ministers arriving in office could adjust all the dials on the departmental dashboard, and completely shift the organisation's focus and emphasis. In practice, ministers cannot pull all the levers at once – the machine will simply seize up and refuse to move. Ministers must therefore be selective about where they choose to apply their effort. The physical and emotional energy to do this even once shouldn't be underestimated. Politicians are lucky to get the chance to pick more than two issues where they can change the weather, and making a success of them both requires being luckier still.

For a digital team to exert enough influence to transform how a government works, the sponsoring minister must consider its success as one of her very highest priorities: number one or two. If she does not choose to spend her political capital on it when things get difficult – and is seen by the organisation not to be spending it – then those happy with the status quo will know they can see the threat of change off without too much bother.

This leads on to the second important quality of good political cover: stability. This, unfortunately, is rarely in anyone's gift but the prime minister or president – and often not even them. Ministerial reshuffles tend to be made for party political reasons, not those of government effectiveness. However, the chances of a digital team embedding itself in the wider organisation are far higher if the political sponsor is secure in their post for several years. Anything less than three years is likely to be insufficient.

The reason for this is obvious. If government ministers are transient figures, anyone with objections to what they are trying to do can simply run down the clock. Delay tactics can be deployed very easily in an organisation that on its best days moves with brick-like fleetness. Regular changes in political leadership tend to set the digital institution back to square one, especially if they happen early in its life. This is partly as a result of the lack of awareness most politicians have of the web. If a new political boss walks in every 18 months with no clear idea of what digital is or what you're trying to do, you spend the first six months of every term making the same basic arguments. Just at the moment they become effective supporters of the team, they're replaced.

A third component of effective political cover is which department the minister is responsible for. Putting responsibility for the first digital team under a minister with a specific policy remit – like justice, say – risks boxing it off. Government departments often believe they are special, and in various ways different from their sibling institutions. Attaching the digital transformation agenda to a specific ministry allows others to say: 'Well, that's all well and good, but it wouldn't work here. Tax is completely different to justice. It's tax! Be reasonable.'

The ideal political cover, therefore, must generally come from a minister responsible for a central ministry. In the UK this was the Cabinet Office; in other jurisdictions, it is often the finance ministry or prime minister's office. In all cases, the institution needs to have the political expectation that it can operate across departments and policy areas, and practical levers to shape departmental behaviour.

Different countries cut their central departments into different pieces, with different power dynamics and leverage over departments. Sometimes the whip hand is determined by the political occupants of the ministerial jobs, other times it is the institutional weight of the organisations themselves. However weak a British Chancellor might be personally, the Treasury will almost always be the first among equals in departmental terms because of the power it has over allocating money. In any case, the political support for a successful digital team needs to be sat in a powerful and aligned centre.

Political cover should not be seen as a necessity for setting up successful digital teams only in governments. Very similar rules operate in large businesses, albeit with the word 'political' read with a small 'p'. Corporates are as burdened with legacy and inertia as governments. Just like ministers, chief executives have a finite limit of places on which to focus their energy and momentum. Like government, executives are regularly shuffled to shore up alliances and sideline threats. Like government, it is extremely difficult to transfer transformation from a business unit to the whole organisation – a strong centre is better placed to work across the group.

Chief Digital Officer

No matter how well placed and enthusiastic your political cover, it is something to be used sparingly. To run the digital institution day to day, you need the right leader on the ground. For them to have a chance of success, they need to be given the right mandate.

There is a very good chance that the right candidate for this job is not currently in your organisation. The role of the Chief Digital Officer (CDO) is that of disruptor-in-chief. Even for an incumbent with a very strong personality, that task is not an easy one. To succeed requires them to openly ask uncomfortable questions about the expectations of an organisation they have already forged a relatively long and successful career in. To some extent, they need to challenge the legitimacy of their own path to win seniority and trust. That's hard to do with credibility. All new CDOs must have the right to ask what seem to be very obvious questions of their employers, because sometimes these turn out not to have good answers. Incumbents may not be given the opportunity to look with truly fresh eyes.

Hiring your CDO from outside carries its own risks. Most large organisations can recall at least one experience of being burned by bringing in outsiders. Often there is fault on both sides. In the UK government at least, there is often the assumption – on both sides of the public/private divide – that a robust injection of corporate best practice is all that's needed to provide a shot-in-the-arm to a lazy, moribund Whitehall. For their part, government officials justifiably resent the idea that someone with no experience of their world can turn up claiming to know all the answers. The more adversarial bureaucrats among them often fail to resist the temptation to make life harder for their new colleagues than it needs to be. More often than not the business people (and, unfortunately, they are mostly businessmen) come prepared for draughts, only for the five-dimensional chessboard to come out. They sprint into the quicksand, with the more tenacious among them guided towards it by senior officials.

Wherever they come from, the prospective CDO must be disruptive without the expectation that the organisation they are joining is (a) full of people who are basically idle and incompetent, and (b) what worked in their old job can simply be cut and pasted into their new one. We have seen several corporate titans turn up in government with exactly these preconceptions, and fail. Talking to their predecessors is a good move for the CDO-elect to make.

Having a clear, open-minded impression of the organisation they're joining is an essential prerequisite for any new senior leader. However, the new CDO must balance a lack of prejudice with a very clear vision for how the organisation should change. The risk of being pragmatic to a fault is that the strong culture of the place you walk into will envelop you entirely. If they don't have something to aim for from the minute you begin the job, the CDO is always likely to be playing catch-up.

All this points to the kind of experience a CDO needs. The best candidates for the role are not necessarily those who have cut their management teeth in digitally native organisations, companies like Google and Amazon created during the internet era. Some executives from these worlds may have only ever worked in a culture largely responsive to the new expectations that the web has set for consumers, citizens and employees alike. Digital natives will not have had to pick fights over uprooting legacy, nor are they necessarily paragons of the working practices that will transfer smoothly into your existing organisation. The leaders likely to most flourish in transforming government will be of the internet era, but understand what preceded it. They have changed the direction of organisations operating with significant amounts of technological and human legacy. They will have replaced old tools and old thinking without killing the company.

The nature of this kind of experience implies a few other essential qualities. They will have a good working knowledge of the technology of the open internet. That doesn't mean they have to be hackers, but they should be able to explain what actually happens when you click on a hyperlink, and what API stands for. They should also espouse the working practices outlined in earlier chapters – agile teams, iterative development, openness – and have proved themselves willing to stick by their staff when times get tough. This last characteristic is perhaps the most important of all.

How senior your CDO needs to be really depends on your organisation's instinct for hierarchy. Most large, old organisations – and all government bureaucracies – still set great store by grades. When government officials introduce themselves to one another, it is typical for them to say, 'I'm the Grade 7 from the Department of Pencils.' Name, rank, serial number; this is the agreed shorthand for how most bureaucracies convey authority. The grade of your CDO actually matters less than their ability to get access to the team's main political sponsor. Nonetheless, for smoothing the path at the official level, pulling rank still matters. Ideally, the CDO needs to have a seat at whatever board level determines the biggest decisions about how the organisation manages itself. In business, that means being on a par with the likes of the chief operating officer or chief finance officer. In government, that typically means they need to rank on a par with the officials charged with running departments. We didn't manage this in the UK, partly because we didn't realise quite how important it was before we started, and partly because some senior officials were decidedly unkeen on the prospect after we did. Other jurisdictions, such Ontario and Peru, have learned from our misstep.

A basic and obvious-sounding point is that the digital institution's leader should be one job, done by one person. In governments and corporates, board-level responsibility for the tasks a digital leader should be expected to handle tend to be scattered far and wide. Accountabilities cut across multiple people and departments. When things go awry, it is unclear who should be carrying the can. The need to combine various jobs and sinecures into a single role can be a useful bargaining chip when negotiating the seniority of the post before the CDO post is advertised.

As a quid pro quo for taking on such a big job, the CDO needs to be given tools that give them a fighting chance of success. When companies and governments make marquee digital and technology hires, defining this mandate and landing it within the organisation is often the missing piece. The best CDO candidate in the world isn't going to get much done with just their great job title.

The first CDO should therefore have unequivocal responsibility for all public-facing digital services on the internet, and the power to direct all government spending on digital. These two powers underpin the CDO's ability to drive change through an organisation at scale. Exactly how to deploy those powers will come later. We talk more about this in chapter 7.

Given the leader's importance and mandate, it may seem counterintuitive to hire the first delivery team before the CDO turns up. In practice, that tends to be the right sequence of events. Most CDO candidates worth their salt will already have plenty of attractive offers on the table, most of them better paid and less exhausting than a post transforming your organisation. They won't want to join you unless you can prove you're serious, and one way to prove you're serious is to have a high-quality group of people already inside the tent delivering high-quality work. However friendly and enthusiastic the politicians wooing them may be, any decent CDO will run a mile from having a day 1 team only composed of policy fixers.

That is not to downplay the fixers' importance. Very little will get done without them.

Bureaucratic hackers

If the product team covered in the previous chapter is your first team, your second team is the bureaucratic hackers. It

69

isn't easy to classify in precise terms what the hackers do, partly because the ground they cover is so wide. In the simplest terms, the hackers are the people who clear a path for the digital delivery teams to deliver the best possible services for users, unblocking the things that would slow them down and avoiding any traps.

Governments and large old companies acquire a lot of baggage. Getting things done in big organisations, especially at below the personal connections that exist at executive levels, often requires a special blend of dogged determination and verve. It also means knowing the unwritten rules of an organisation, be they complicated processes, the right people to talk to or the appropriate etiquette for approaching certain questions.

While the digital team is there to act as an agent of change for the organisation, that does not mean it has carte blanche to be ignorant of the current rules, much less rip up or ignore them all. If you go back to first principles, many of the most frustrating aspects of working in a bureaucracy – the paperwork, the delays, the acronyms and language – are grounded in perfectly reasonable intent. Often there are very good legal, security or moral reasons lying behind the way things are. The problem arises when wise intent is smothered by many layers of abstraction. As experienced hands within the organisation, the job of the bureaucratic hackers is to the get to the bottom of the intent behind the rules, explain this to the digital incomers, and ensure that the new teams follow them to everyone's satisfaction. Over time, the hackers can steadily push for replacing the rules and processes for alternatives, on the basis that the digital institution has now proven (rather than just claimed) that they are simpler, clearer and faster at meeting the original intent.

There are many different areas where an ability to go back to first principles in the interests of speed are of invaluable aid to the digital team. These range from the small things – knowing which corporate form-filling exercises are non-negotiable, and which can be safely put to the bottom of the pile, for example – to fundamental enablers of digital transformation: buying products and services from suppliers and other activities brigaded under the world of procurement; recruiting, rewarding and managing the performance of staff, plus the other challenges of HR; understanding what security protections are proportionate, and who is a trusted arbiter of that trade-off. You can't safely challenge the prevailing way these things are done without understanding the reasons why they work that way in the first place.

In government, the ability to understand and navigate the arcane world of policy and winning 'clearance' is paramount. If you can't get agreement to things that need to be signed up to by the whole of the organisation through official channels, you are effectively stuck as a digital team. Equally, if you manage to do this at a far higher pace than is typically expected, you won't achieve the pace of delivery you need to prove the benefits of digital transformation. There is a huge amount of skill and emotional intelligence involved in getting this right; knowing how to engage ministers' private staff, which committees you must go to, how the papers should be written, to whom you speak to square off beforehand, when to make your pitch. The work of the GDS's bureaucratic hackers was less visible and often less heralded than the public-facing services that reached users. It shouldn't have been. Their work often anticipated the most dangerous blockers before they happened, and quietly fixed those that were unavoidable.

The best bureaucratic hackers are calm, angry people. Not uncontrollably angry people – directionless rage at the organisation you work for is not a productive state. Nor do you want people who feel weary and defeated, those who have seen all the organisation's dysfunctions before and conclude: 'Well, it's typical, but what can you do?' You need intelligent, canny people who have worked for the institution long enough to know that it could be a lot better than it currently is, and are passionate enough to challenge the things they believe are holding it back.

First 100 days

Having done the groundwork to form a protective shell around a rapidly moving delivery team, the three to six months that follow are the period when the digital institution can move at its very fastest. The team should move so quickly that by the time any potential objectors have noticed the biggest changes, there's no longer a discussion to be had.

Pretending that changing the way government operates is like a military campaign is a little silly, but there are some common strategic traits. Though you often hear of careless haste in conflict, strategic skill has never been associated with long delays. And claiming territory – or, to be more precise, claiming a mandate to be the legitimate decision maker on certain parts of government business – is something you have to do quickly, preferably before anyone (including yourself, sometimes) has recognised the implications. In an exchange that went down in early GDS legend, a government chief information officer of long standing dismissed the new digital team as 'tinsel'. Without a clear mandate behind it, he might have been right.

One of the more endearing qualities of organisations with long-fixed rules and conventions is that, provided you turn up to meetings and speak with a firm, polite tone, most people will assume you know what you're talking about, and have been given permission by some higher power to get on with doing the things you say need to be done. In some bureaucracies, a burst of decisiveness can be as refreshing as it is unexpected. 'That woman seems to be very sure that this board needs to be closed down, and if she says the boss agrees, I suppose we'd better pack up.' This superpower is a time-bound quality – people eventually work out what you're doing, and really dig their heels in – but it is invaluable early on. Use it to clear as much nonsense out of your way as possible.

The primary objective for the CDO's first 100 days, having brought together digital delivery teams with bureaucratic hackers, should be to clearly set the team's future mandate in a way that sets a course for tackling the structural barriers to digital change, and make sure the wider organisation knows that this is how it is going to be. The new CDO should prioritise a small number of tasks to get things moving the right way.

Setting the right culture

Culture is a strange mix of conscious decisions and unpredictable alchemy of people thrown together. Getting it right brings huge benefits; getting it wrong can spell disaster. The UK government's digital culture was often summed up by the symbols that every visitor remarked upon: the bunting hung all over the office, the stand-up meetings where presenters faced heckling for failing to explain any acronyms, the cakes, the jeans, the monthly GDS all-staff meetings to celebrate successes. The same recipe was later taken out to government offices all over the country, where digital teams fought with estates managers over whether putting sticky notes on walls represented a health and safety risk – and won. Culture manifested as workspaces where someone was more likely to walk over and ask a question than send an email. From the start, the GDS deliberately set a difficult cultural tone to the organisation it was part of – it was proudly (and some said arrogantly) different, open and combative. Nobody could miss the fact that the digital institution was setting itself apart. That didn't always meet with approval, especially when digital teams were criticised for lacking empathy with those working in a more typical bureaucratic world. Work hard to create a culture, not a culture war.

Defining and recruiting the digital institution's leadership team

Just as hiring a product team quickly is generally impossible to do through the normal routes, your standard recruitment processes are unlikely to be adequate for finding other leaders. Establishing the norm early on that you will reshape the standard process to get the people you need, legally and openly, is important. The big medium-term advantage of doing this is setting a precedent for other departments to use the same loopholes you have created. Others will appreciate you creating a space that allows them to bring in better people, provided you make it as easy for them to use as you.

Bring disparate threads and teams together

Large organisations often end up with several separate teams working simultaneously on very similar issues. This is inefficient, but the more insidious productivity problem is worse: duplication stokes a kind of perverse competition, endless 'coordination' meetings and turf-war arguments.

In organisations not yet comfortable with digital working, the chances are that several teams will have responsibility for different bits of the digital and technology agenda. Restructuring those teams to put them under one roof with one leader and line of accountability cuts through much of this noise. The GDS was an amalgam of six different teams spread across three different departments. The CDO mustn't let perfect be the enemy of the good when pushing for consolidation; big organisations and governments will always be fragmented. Focus on removing the obvious doubling-up.

Move all delivery teams to co-located accommodation where agile working is easily possible

You know how sometimes you turn up at a new place and just instantly fall for it, knowing that however long you spend there won't be enough? Your digital team's office won't be like that. The GDS's first home looked like what it was: an unloved government building with no single owner, filled with desks bound for charity clearance and decorated by distracted contractors out of whatever materials could be justified in the event of a trouble-making Freedom of Information request. As long as it has desks, walls, windows and a good internet connection, everyone can fit in it, and you can make reasonable changes whenever you like, that will do – provided co-located teams can work together.

Writing a 'Hello World' blog post[43]

Government officials are not expected – or even allowed, in many cases – to talk to people from the outside world, and journalists in particular. Companies concerned about commercial confidentiality tend to impose similar restrictions. All interactions with the press must be made through a designated communications team. The aim of that team tends to be ensuring that the team says as little as possible, and, if forced to speak, that it is not saying anything too interesting. Talking to people in an open and relatively approachable way is part of doing digital properly, so getting agreement to run separate digital channels and post information without several layers of clearance is a must. Most senior officials and executives will instinctively feel this is an unnecessary risk. Persuading (and then showing) them otherwise should be high on the CDO's first agenda, making clear that the blog is the team's primary internal and external comms channel.

One reading of this list risks painting the new CDO as the drunk who walks into an unfamiliar pub and takes a swing at the whole bar. In an ideal world, there will be no need for any arguments at all. A well-judged charm offensive might win the day. If you're lucky, other corporate functions like the HR and finance teams that these five tasks bump up against may be delighted to come onboard and test out a different way of doing things. They may have wanted an excuse or the permission to do so for years, but weren't lucky enough to get the fortunate circumstances that have landed in the digital team's lap.

However, it's likely that only a lonely handful in each function will be exactly the angry types you'll need for scaling up your bureaucratic hackers. There's a reason organisations haven't already sorted out the problems the CDO is trying to overcome. In the toughest cases, an entire division will hate you for challenging their orthodoxy, and fight every step of the way. In this scenario, compromises are inevitable, but not capitulation. Giving in is dangerous; if your digital institution fails to get reasonable control over your hiring, workspace, communications, structure and purpose, the room you'll have for manoeuvre in the months ahead will be far more limited.

In parallel with these 'hard' steps that give several un-equivocal messages to other functions in the organisation, the first 100 days is also the time for a CDO and the collective digital team to establish the peer relationships that generate soft power. Holding face-to-face meetings with all the top officials and ministers who will be key partners in the first year is a must for the new CDO.

Of course, one of the best ways to win friends and influence people is to give them things they want that they've never been able to get before, especially if it makes them look good. The GDS enjoyed an early coup when it built Prime Minister David Cameron an app that allowed him to show off about the success of Tech City at a major conference – and by implication show that his officials were capable of keeping pace with the start-ups. Finding out exactly how to please your future trickiest customers is not a bad way of spending your first few months.

Winning friends internally is far from enough though. Much more importantly, it is now time for people outside the bubble of your organisation to start seeing the difference.

SUMMARY

- Digital delivery cannot succeed without team members who deeply understand the organisation, from the minister/CEO level down. Bring insiders in from the start.
- Stories of digital change often leave out the bureaucratic hacking needed in the background. You can't change anything for good without those skills on the team.

- A CDO must be highly literate in the technologies and practices of the internet era, and given a strong mandate to operate across the whole organisation.
- Make the most of your CDO's first 100 days; there will never be the chance to move so fast again.

Chapter 6

Building credibility

Your fledgling new digital institution is well set, with a clear sense of how it will work, and teams are up and running. All that needs to be done now is to actually ship some products. If you can't do that, it's time to pack up and go home. While it is not easy to get to this point, none of what has happened so far has made a real difference to the people who really matter – citizens or customers, your users.

Delivery is so important because it is the thing that many big organisations have forgotten how to do well. Showing that it can be done – simpler, cheaper and faster than anything the organisation has seen for many years – is the only thing that will really make the argument for digital change credible in the debates to come.

Beware the innovation trap

It is at this point where digital institutions have to differentiate themselves from 'innovation units'. Later in this chapter, we will come to a type of innovation team that is well worth having. However, as a general rule 'innovation' is something to be cautious about.

Innovation units are an increasingly common sight in governments and large corporates. They set up with a remit to be disruptive, in much the same way that a digital unit should be. Many innovation units are full of good people and smart ideas. They often take on a similar working culture and practices those described in previous chapters: agile, multi-disciplinary and open. However, the risk of bracketing disruption under the banner of innovation is that it can ultimately remain peripheral to the business, something to be held at arm's length from whatever the 'real work' is. Many innovation teams find themselves trapped in the purgatory of being an add-on to the day to day rather than a force charged with fundamentally reshaping the organisation.

This is one of those cases where language matters. The word 'innovation' might have been rendered flat and lifeless to some by its endless use in glossy presentations, but it still sounds dynamic, exciting and new to certain ears. The problem for some teams that have innovation in their name is that the name turns out to be the most innovative thing about them. Creating things that are less than they seem through clever naming is a well-worn tactic of big organisations; the more go-faster stripes a name has, the deeper the conventionality lying underneath.

The thing is, innovation, by definition, will always be separate and different from what the rest of government or the business does most of the time. Innovation teams are destined to always run one step ahead of the rest of the organisation, and are not incentivised to help everyone catch up with them. How can you be 'innovative' if everyone is doing the same thing as you?

The other, linked problem with innovation units is that they rarely actually get down to the business of building things that reach users. This sounds like a sweeping and maybe unfair statement, so it's worth explaining. Innovation units tend to be staffed by designers and thinkers who are capable of producing (often very impressive) presentations and proto-types. Some of those prototypes do get tested on real people. But they rarely achieve the velocity needed to get out of the innovation unit and into the organisation proper, replacing or augmenting an existing service. To do that, the team respon-sible for the new services needs to be able to get into the guts of the organisation's operations – the IT spaghetti, frontline staff, and so on – and make changes. Few innovation units achieve enough influence or leverage within the wider organ-isation to make that happen. Arguably, by having shown that things could be done differently, they have done their job whether or not the business bothers to put the theory into practice.

In some places – particularly government bureaucracies – innovation units are tolerated because they fit the Hitchhik-er's Guide's description of Earth: 'mostly harmless'. They are allowed to persist by the hierarchies threatened by disruption because they don't really challenge the status quo, merely point out that alternative paths are available. As a quid pro quo, those who would be threatened by actual delivery loudly applaud the impressive yet innocuousness work of the inno-vation unit's output as ground-breaking and valuable. A cynic might say that innovation units offer a happy equilibrium in organisations that don't actually want to change very much. Happy that is, for everyone except the organisation's users.

Choosing your first service

To avoid the innovation trap, you need to build something – and something sufficiently integral to what the organisation does on a daily basis for it to matter.

In the UK, two services provided the initial proving ground for the GDS: GOV.UK, a website for publishing information that would replace the 2,000-plus separate websites managed by the government with a single domain, and e-petitions, an entirely new service commissioned by parliament to allow any UK citizen to submit a formal petition.

This does not mean that any government or business contemplating digital transformation should necessarily pick two programmes like these as their starting point – they just happened to be the best candidates for the GDS at that time. A few factors made them good places to start.

Greenfield

In many ways, taking on the e-petitions service could have been a very bad idea for the GDS. The idea was to create a new service that would allow anyone to submit an online petition to parliament. It came as a result of an unexpected announcement from the Speaker of the House of Commons, apparently demob happy on his last day in post, rather than through the more typical party manifesto route. It also came with a very public deadline. Neither of these are ideal conditions for a new project. There was no avoiding it though. Here was the promise of a new digital service just after the creation of a digital team. The GDS had to put its hand up.

What made e-petitions workable, apart from the incredible work of the team managing to turn around a fully working service used by thousands of people within 12 weeks, was that it posed a clearly bounded need that had few connections to other bits of government business. There were no legacy technology systems to worry about, no other teams in government who claimed responsibility for doing something identical already, no accretion of laws or regulations to meet. E-petitions was pretty much a blank sheet of paper. Even better, the team could use lessons learned from the previous, abandoned version of an online petitions service built by Number 10 with the help of the same civic technology community who now found themselves working in the GDS.

The e-petitions service proved incredibly popular. In the first 100 days after it went live, an average of 18 people signed a petition every minute. 21,500 petitions were submitted for consideration, with 6 of them reaching the threshold of 100,000 signatures that triggered a parliamentary debate. Not long afterwards, the White House announced they would launch a US online petitions service – 'We the People' – nodding their acknowledgement to the UK team's work as a source of inspiration.

Because it was greenfield, the e-petitions team could focus all of its energies on coming up with the best possible answer to meeting the user need, rather than delicately balancing egos and opinions of colleagues elsewhere. A fresh opportunity like this is a rare luxury in government. At some point, most bureaucracies have tried most things. For almost any topic or policy you can name, somewhere there is drawer with a file in it that says 'we tried that once before, and it didn't work'.

Over time, the GDS became drawn in to picking more brownfield services as exemplars of digital transformation. These were instances where many of the crucial policy and technology decisions (such as selecting particular software, or determining certain policy rules) had already been taken long before the digital team got involved. Despite the heroics of many people in departments working alongside a GDS transformation unit to see many of these through to a successful delivery, it was impossible to deliver them all. In hindsight, we shouldn't have taken on the overhaul of so many services where the teams on the ground had limited control over the biggest choices defining the future direction of the project. Be wary of brownfield, especially early on.

Simple

If you get the chance to create a simple digital service for something genuinely new, grab it with both hands. Simple is an important word here; there is no sense in embarking on a wholescale reform of the welfare system or setting up a fully electronic driving licence as your first project. Governments and large businesses love complexity. Avoid the temptation.

If the business strategy or government manifesto is not bursting with opportunities offering bounded originality, a good place to look is the small tasks where your current structures are forcing people to come up with workarounds. One of the first mini-services created on GOV.UK was a page that showed when the next national bank holiday was. It was easy, searched for millions of times a year, yet there wasn't a single, easily found official answer anywhere on the web.

Visible

The great advantage of doing something that is technically and intellectually simple is that it should be difficult to get wrong. The prevailing expectation most people have of government online services is that they will be terrible experiences, if they work at all. With a low risk of disappointment or failure, you can comfortably ratchet up the number of people exposed to the new service without too much risk.

One of the more powerful insights from the GDS experience was the different perspectives of government officials and users on simplicity. Fixing a bank holiday page was barely worthy of note to an official – just too straightforward to comment on. These very clever people, often in possession of an exhaustive view on a particular policy problem, would sometimes struggle to see the wood for the trees. However, for the millions of people who saved a couple of minutes clicking across multiple pages to find the information they wanted, it was a little, obvious but pleasing improvement. It wasn't worth a letter to *The Times*, it was just good. Good digital work is a million silent nods of approval, not one loud round of applause.

To make the equation work, it is right to aim high for the public exposure of your early work. Over the first 100 days of e-petitions 18 people signed every minute, on average. The e-petitions service was also a goldmine for journalists – a million people signing a petition asking for Jeremy Clarkson to be appointed prime minister is an easy story for every newspaper – increasing interest further. Equally importantly, from a technical design point of view, those visits were likely to arrive in large spikes. Being able to cope smoothly with heavy demands was a clear user need for the new service, and exactly the kind of eventuality that government services tended to fail on.

If the service had fallen over from weight of traffic, it would have caused brief embarrassment for the government. More importantly, however, it would land a near-fatal blow to the digital team's ability to say that it represented a departure from the typical record of public sector IT. That e-petitions didn't experience a familiar kind of public IT failure on a grand scale was itself enough for it to stand out as a success.

To get a sense of just how visible a service will be, you will ideally need access to data. The web traffic logs on existing websites should give you some indication, as will call centre data. However, for completely greenfield services, there may be no historical numbers to work from. In these cases, you will have to calibrate potential visibility with a combination of your instincts and the amount of political attention the new idea is getting. Plan for worst-case scenarios, and run exercises that put the service through its paces. There should be no surprises on the day it goes live.

Reuseable

When you strip away the nuances, an awful lot of government business largely boils down to a small number of processes and transactions. As a leading UK service designer has put it, most of government is mostly service design, most of the time.[44] That approximation still leaves a great deal of government business that doesn't slot into neat piles, and there's plenty of variation within each broad category of services. Getting a fishing licence is a different prospect to getting a driving licence. However, it holds up as a broad principle.

There are many things that governments and other large organisations do badly in many different ways, when it would be far cheaper and better for users to do it once and well. For the purposes of early project selection, you should keep one eye on whether the thing you are building is offering a template that can be easily reused at scale across the organisation.

From the beginning, GOV.UK was designed as a publishing platform – a platform being something that a whole range of actors can make use of without needing to start from scratch.

Platforms are the bedrock of digitally native companies. eBay, Alibaba and Amazon are retail platforms that allow anyone to sell their goods there; AirBnB is an accommodation platform, Uber a transactions platform, and so on. Much as the world's biggest shops now hold almost no stock of their own, GOV.UK is the largest publisher of UK government information despite the central team writing only a tiny percentage of the words.

Other services will offer opportunities to build widgets that can be copy and pasted into other projects later. If you're taking payments, or building a store finder, or an appointments booking tool, all of those things will be needed again somewhere.

Starting your delivery with the presumption you will make your code open is the right thing to do, bearing in mind that parts of your service could be the first components in a toolbox used by future teams. A word of caution though. The risk of building everything to be ready for an unknown future is that it encourages a form of dangerous perfectionism. In the early days, it is more important to build good services that ship even if they don't translate easily into common components. A service made of near-perfect parts that never actually sees the light of day is the most imperfect service of all.

Do less

Even after applying these four tests to selecting your delivery priorities, there is a very good chance you will be left with several potential project candidates in the mix. These will be joined by a few other ideas that don't really meet the criteria but are difficult to shake off.

Striking the right level of delivery ambition at the outset is a difficult judgment. Adopting agile ways of working and hiring talented specialists confer a lot of momentum on a new digital institution, but it doesn't allow it to ignore the trade-off every team has to make between quality, quantity and time. You may have bought a little more capacity, but time travel is still impossible.

While there is no definitive right answer to getting this balance right, the thing for a new digital team to consider in its formative stages is how to define itself as distinct from the mediocre record that precedes it. The overwhelming expectation of IT, in the UK and most other parts of the world, is that it will be slow, expensive and deliver poor outcomes for users. On the other hand, not many people would argue that IT is in short supply. In other words, the traditional big IT philosophy has spent a couple of decades turning the quantity up to 11, and tried to avoid looking too closely at the quality or time dials. Large organisations, and governments especially, tend to fall into the trap of thinking that they are bigger than they really are. This happens no matter how large the country or region in question is. This delusion leads to the idea that buying loads of complicated technology is therefore 'normal'. To get past that, the self-perception of large organisations has to change. Strip away all the pomp and history, and few government services do anything significantly more complicated than an online dating site.

A digital institution should therefore make it part of its mission to do less. To overcome the legitimate scepticism about what it is trying to do, the new team needs to focus on producing a small number of excellent services, and quickly. As time goes on, the team can and should calibrate this balance to deliver more things, over a longer period of time (though this is much easier said than done).

Good gatekeeping

If the digital team were left in a bubble, sticking to the mantra of doing less would be straightforward. However, news about success, and especially unexpected success, spreads quickly. Once you've begun to deliver services that manage to not only work but look good, people will beat a path to your door.

Many of these suitors will be people who don't quite understand what the digital team is there for yet, but are desperate for a helping hand in finishing their website. Some will assume this new digital team is just the IT shop with a new name, and looking for help putting together a list of requirements to hand over to suppliers.

In these cases, the only option open to you is to say 'no' as politely as possible. After a certain point, being open to all these requests is the most unhelpful thing you can do – you'll be too swamped to deliver your own services properly, much less theirs too.

One of the biggest challenges faced by agile teams is that no service should ever be considered finished. There is always room and user need for making incremental tweaks and improvements. As time goes on, the digital team will build up a growing list of products and services it needs to maintain and improve. Learning how to say no – to your own teams as much as to those outside the institution – is therefore imperative, and an essential lesson for the team's survival and sustainability.

Governments and large organisations being what they are, there are some people – prime ministers, presidents, CEOs – that you can't say no to. If you're lucky enough to have them calling on you, the pressing challenge is how to effectively handle their requests. This is especially tricky if what they are asking for happens to fail several of the criteria for sensibly picking services.

Faced with this, a good tactic is to set up a product team entirely separate from those charged with delivering your small number of chosen flagship services. The latter can then be left alone to get on with building something that serves as the best illustration of the institution's approach. The separate product team spends its time fielding requests from the fickle characters up in the gods. This role of running interference and protecting delivery is quite different from those working on full services, so you should give them a different name. Now is the time to resurrect the word 'innovation'.

Innovation is the right name for this team, because it is a truer reflection of what they are doing. In the GDS, it was also known as the fireworks team. Producing brief, colourful impressive displays is at the heart of what their customers really want. It is a lazy stereotype to say that most senior executives only have time to engage with surface-level improvement. Even so, it is true enough to say that if a CEO or politician has a choice between seeing 80% of the benefit of an idea they plucked out of thin air in four weeks versus 90% of the benefit in six months, they'll pick the former every time.

Say a prime minister asks for a digital dashboard to display hospital waiting time data. The innovation team should have the skills required to build a beautiful working prototype that appears to function like a fully functioning service. This is theatre; it won't be too sophisticated under the surface. That doesn't matter. If the PM decides she wants that having seen the prototype, then the hard work to re-prioritise the team's work around building a robust product can begin with the reassurance of a very clear ask from the top. But if the PM is happy with just the elegant front-end put in front of her after a month's work, then the digital team has proved their worth, cheaply, quickly and without interrupting the deeper delivery work going on elsewhere. The credibility that brings is powerful currency for later.

Is this a disingenuous approach? No, unless you plan on pretending that your prototype is a fully functioning service when presenting it to the CEO – which is not a good idea. There is no harm in honest humility from the innovation team, in saying that what you have produced can be improved upon, and that the CEO meeting is a crucial piece of user testing to determine whether it is worth pursuing further. There is no difference between putting a working prototype in front of the minister and giving him a draft report to comment on. Except for one thing: the prototype can get telling feedback in seconds, while the report takes hours, days or weeks.

Scaling teams

Once you have begun to deliver significant frontline digital services, there will be increased pressure on the team to grow. Quite quickly, there will simply be too many hypotheses to test or relationships to manage for any one product team.

The typical bureaucratic response to scale pressures is closely related to the organisation's relationship with risk. Bigger services with more users have higher stakes. Lots of governments and businesses try to mitigate the risks by talking them death, adding more layers of management and governance to the mix. This places a great overhead of paperwork on the team, slows down delivery and ultimately doesn't protect from the biggest risk of all – actually making sure something useful ends up in front of users.

Part of the reason why this happens is because of the divide that exists between strategy and delivery. As a service becomes bigger, absorbing more resources and reaching more users, it also becomes more important to the organisation. Policymakers who consider themselves the most important people in the room elbow their way in, often in large numbers. The voices that guided the service's early development based on data, user insight and operational knowledge become diluted or disappear altogether.

Rather than adding more management, the best way to scale digital teams is to scale the unit of delivery to cope with discrete tasks as they arise. This means replicating the product teams. As a digital service gets more complex, you should add more multidisciplinary product teams with a mix of skills and perspectives to add complementary problems. The teams should be loosely coupled, but tightly aligned to meeting the needs of the same users. Crucially, these teams will include people with deep knowledge of frontline operations who can provide insights based on reality. This is not a quality traditionally associated with the layers of management that tend to accompany the process of scaling up a service.

One of the things overlooked by organisations trying to adopt agile, iterative approaches is the need to apply the same discipline to their team structure as they do to whatever service they are building. As teams scale and grow, they need to keep having regular conversations with themselves that ensure they are still testing hypotheses about the best way for them to work together. Regular retrospective meetings that devote time to working through what a team is doing well and not so well are a good, structured route to getting better.

SUMMARY

- Be careful about describing yourself as 'innovators'; the digital teams should be working at the heart of an organisation, not on the periphery.
- Pick a first major project that is greenfield, simple, visible and maximises learning.
- Stand up a team to manage important requests that distract from your main focus.
- Ensure the rhetoric does not outpace reality, and learn to say no.

Chapter 7

Winning the arguments

It is the Balkanisation of authority across government that is
responsible for dysfunctional decision-making.

— Nick Clegg, Deputy Prime Minister (2010–15)

The focus of a digital team shifts over time. Sometimes the
primary objective should be creating the conditions for
the team to do the right thing. At other times, it will be using
those conditions to actually deliver improved experiences for
users. Once you've created space for a team to succeed, they
can get on with shipping small, fast and bold products and
services. The more ambitious the aims of a digital organisation become, the more conditions they need to put in place
to have a chance of releasing greater benefits.

These two tasks – building things and creating the space
to build things – can run happily in parallel once a team is up
and running. The whole digital team should not be pivoting
from one to another; your product teams will focus on the
delivery, the bureaucratic hackers on clearing a path to advance. What will change is the issue that is front and centre
for the digital institutions' leadership. Calibrating the balance
between healthy delivery and clearing space for moving on
to bigger things at any given moment is one of the trickiest
judgement calls. Stay too attached to delivery, and you risk
curtailing your ability to build a truly digital organisation. Fly

DIGITAL TRANSFORMATION AT SCALE

too far off into the distance, and you may lose track of actually delivering improvements to both users and the bottom line. As they are the benefits of creating a better organisation in the first place, you forget them at your peril.

The temptation that new digital teams encounter is for them to try and line up a perfect scenario for a successful digital organisation to take flight in one go. You might come away from reading this book thinking, 'What's the point in beginning anything without having first sorted out the best staff, the perfect political conditions, the right organisational culture, and had all the most obvious blockers swept aside?' If all that were ticked off, you could surely then accelerate as fast as you can into the space you've created, delivering more impressive and impactful things for users, and saving money more quickly. This sounds very sensible. The only problem is it will never happen. The chances of creating a perfect environment for changing an old, legacy-driven organisation – and holding that scenario steady in an ever-changing, event-driven world – are zero. One of the biggest mistakes we have seen new digital institutions make is waiting until they can see the very bottom of the pool before diving in from the highest board. Taking a shallow dive into murkier waters is the wiser way to go.

Digital teams should feel comfortable (or at least, get used to feeling uncomfortable) with working things out as they go along. Win arguments as they arise. There is no perfect end point for a digital organisation to aspire to. In the UK government, the digital team tried to win the most important arguments that were in front of it at the time. At many times, the strategic question confronting us was very simple. Mat Wall, a GDS technical architect, summed it up: 'What can we fix to help our teams ship better products this Friday than last week?' Having your strategic priorities led by what is blocking delivery and meeting user needs right now (rather than some unspecified point in the future) is a good way to maintain focus. This week's delivery niggles are a valuable source of suggestions for where to invest the efforts of the bureaucratic hackers that can fix them.

The first set of conditions that need putting in place for a new digital institution to work are largely about making sure that a new kind of organisation, capable of agile, user-centred delivery, can be transplanted into a large bureaucracy without tissue rejection. We explained these in chapter 1: these are the four things that give a digital team the licence to simply make a start.

After putting those in place, most digital teams will then go through a period of successfully delivering a certain kind of output; small, low-risk and greenfield projects of the type we spoke about in chapter 5. These are projects that can exist and thrive independently from the legacies – technological and cultural – that are attached to the wider organisation. However, as the digital team turns to look at redesigning services that are deeply embedded within the various tendrils of the existing organisations – the brownfield sites – it quickly becomes obvious that the conditions that allowed a digital team to exist are not enough to transform the whole business. Creating the environment for this kind of change to start happening required the digital team to acquire a new mandate, and win a new set of arguments.

From the centre and here to help

You will not be able to effect change within a government machine or large corporate body if you cannot operate levers of influence from a central position. This leverage over the various parts that make up the whole organisation, be they government departments or subsidiary businesses, is critical. The levers must allow the digital team to consistently modify behaviour and overcome inertia. If your digital institution has reached the stage of delivering new products and services relatively easily but has no leverage over the existing legacy, it is probably time to prioritise creating a stronger cross-organisational mandate.

Mandate is one of those slippery, dangerous terms. It means different things to different people. From a department's perspective, one reading of the paragraph above is that a central body – such as a finance ministry or strategy team – should be handed the power to dictate terms to the rest of the organisation about anything they feel like. That is not what we're saying.

Mandates vary in two ways. They can operate through a different mix of powers; some combination of soft (via influence, personal relationships, exchanges of favours and shared best practice) and hard levers (laws or decrees, rules, spending controls). They can also vary according to the range of issues that the mandate covers; recruitment, money, technology choices, legal frameworks, and so on. The mandate your digital institution needs depends on the organisation you are working in.

In the UK, we took the decision to create a relatively broad mandate with a set of hard levers for the GDS. The digital team needed to be able to administer stiff medicine in order to overcome entrenched interests within and outside government. These interests prevented parts of the civil service from delivering services that either met user needs or represented a reasonable investment of taxpayers' money.

That decision was made partly based on the experience of others. Previous attempts at reform with a powerless or non-existent centre struggled to make any sustained progress. This is a reform problem, not a digital problem. Other attempts to change the rhythm and shape of institutions have faced similar problems; it took 26 years, two major ministerial reviews and an intervention from Winston Churchill to give statistics its rightful place in government.[45]

Not everyone agreed with our judgement. Some complained that the GDS's central mandate unreasonably diminished their department's organisational power. However, whatever the exact nature of a digital's team influence over the collective organisation, having some form of central mandate appears to be essential in driving savings and improvements to the digital experience for users. We have yet to find a compelling example of an organisation that has successfully transformed itself from a legacy-driven business without some form of central push.

Other organisations and governments – particularly those that are younger and carry less historical and cultural baggage than Britain's bureaucracy, 150 years old in its current form – will not require so adversarial a central mandate to drive change. We have seen large, legacy-ridden corporate conglomerates achieve a huge amount of digital change largely through having trusted digital leaders working in the centre who win the trust of their fellow executives. The mandate the central team has in this case is largely implicit in their soft influence; departments follow a central team if and when they recognise it is the expert. It also helps if the chief executive publicly makes it very clear that she believes the centre is the expert too. Giving a digital team a central mandate does not mean it has to be combative.

It is easy to ascribe the inertia of bureaucracies to natural forces, uncontrollable by individuals. This is not true. It takes surprisingly few individuals to completely gum up a huge government machine. Not many people are obstructive for the sheer hell of it. In most cases they will have very good personal or professional reasons to maintain the status quo. When your digital team turns up to upend their position, they will hide, delay or fight. Faced with this, influence, charm and friendly wheedling may only get you so far. Teams trying to start digital institutions (especially in governments) therefore shouldn't underestimate the value of acquiring hard powers. You don't get many chances to ask for them, and they are much more easily removed than conferred.

To get that hold of an expanded mandate, you need to make the most of your opportunities. After two years, the GDS was invited to present what had been achieved in digital government to a Cabinet meeting – an extremely rare privilege. Demonstrating new digital services meant getting a TV into the Cabinet room, and persuading Number 10 that this didn't represent a threat to national security. Having managed that, we took the chance to make some very clear asks of the country's most senior politicians. By presenting the proposed mandate alongside the progress already made, no one was about to get in the way.

Deciding the right balance of hard and soft power is a choice that you can shape according to the organisation around you. The scope of your mandate – the areas of the business that the digital institution gains the right to shape and judge – should be determined by what is blocking delivery. Again, this will vary from place to place. However, there are some issues where a cross-organisation mandate is always useful in managing the hard conversations to come.

Wrangling IT

Digital and IT often have a troubled relationship. IT, in the form it tends to take in large organisations, is technology that has been conceived with a mindset that predates or ignores the open internet. This sets it up in direct opposition to digital.

IT, like laws and regulations, is used by organisations as a sweeping excuse for why the user experience of online services is so poor, and why an organisation can't behave as the digital institution it apparently wants to be. Those who are most often guilty of this dissembling tend to be the people who have the weakest understanding of IT. In some institutions, pinning the woes on the IT department is an article of faith. Relying on ancient back-end systems does naturally make things difficult, but nobody is forcing the organisation to use them. Treating IT as a fixed constraint, as opposed to something that the organisation can make an informed strategic choice about ignoring or prioritising, allows too many senior managers to blame the IT when the real problem is much closer to home.

Regardless of the personalities involved, there are three common reasons for the relationship between IT and digital being rocky: misunderstanding, mythology and contracts.

Misunderstanding may creep in as a consequence of your organisation believing digital is just another way of doing IT. 'You make websites don't you? You must be another IT team.' The existing IT team doesn't want another group muscling in on their patch. A depressingly high number of managers, public and private, are obsessed with 'turf' and their sphere of influence; IT managers are no different. They are generally not inclined to welcome a bunch of upstarts who have turned up uninvited to criticise what they're doing.

Many IT teams in big organisations have got used to nobody really understanding what they do, especially at a senior level. They are unloved – which is unfair – but they are also essentially unaccountable. This can lead to some unhealthy complacency. By having the technical skills to be able to ask the right questions of IT colleagues, digital teams pose a threat to a quiet life. This is not a good place from which to begin a healthy working relationship.

IT security offers another seam of mythology, providing a rich seam of questionable reasons for why things can't possibly be changed. At their worst, security myths actually lead to organisations taking on bigger risks – forced to rely on unusable old technology at work for fear of being hacked, staff eventually turn to unsecured personal devices to get things done.

RETROSPECTIVE: SECURE STATISTICS

The UK Office of National Statistics (ONS) was long an organisation stuck under a digital cloud. Despite having some very able people working in it, the ONS was running an online presence described as 'the worst website in the world' by the *Financial Times*. For most organisations, this would be an embarrassment. For the ONS, a public body with publications that moved markets, it was a deeper worry.

Security mythology contributed to ONS's woes. ONS was obliged to publish certain key economic statistics, such as inflation numbers, at a certain precise time. Many numbers needed to be published at 9 a.m. sharp; not a minute later, as the market demanded them on the dot, and not a minute earlier, as they were embargoed until that moment. Built on creaking old IT, the website's frailties meant that statistics uploaded at 9 a.m. – as the rules decreed – were often not viewable until several minutes afterwards. These delays

---

were earning the ONS some very powerful critics. Fear of security breaches, ill-informed box ticking and lack of basic technology capability had prevented any solutions coming forward.

To unblock the impasse, ONS brought in a national security expert. He gently but firmly explained that provided the numbers were securely encrypted, they could be uploaded to the site hours before. On the stroke of 9, the encryption could be removed – the job of a second. It was a simple solution, but one that could only be reached by framing technology as an enabler of meeting user needs, not as something fixed and unchanging.

As a consequence of outsourcing, many IT teams in big organisations have been effectively captured by suppliers. Denuded of their own technical capabilities, they have been reduced to the role of contract managers – buying things in the hope it will fix the problems caused by the last order of stuff they bought. Without the skills needed to properly interrogate suppliers' offerings, organisations buy the wrong things on lengthy contracts, leaving minimal room for them to respond when circumstances change. All this is anathema to designing and running decent digital services or meet user needs.

It is often difficult to redesign or transform a digital service without tying it back in some way to the legacy IT. To have a chance of success, a digital mandate must make it possible to stop poorly conceived, hugely expensive and long IT contracts from being let. It must also ensure people with genuine technical knowledge are given the opportunity to interrogate new investments in IT; and ask the basic questions that may not have been raised in decades. Good IT managers will embrace the chance to bring new skills into their teams and have the business pay them some proper attention for once. Bad ones will resent the oversight and stick doggedly to ploughing their own furrows.

All of this requires an organisation to stop looking at IT as the dull, frustrating systems that constrain the decisions they can make, and instead consider what technology is needed to support the ever-changing needs of their customers, employees or citizens.

One of the most important technology concepts to embed within your organisation is the idea of technology as a commodity. In simple terms, this is the idea that many building blocks of digital services are relatively inexpensive, widely available and more or less interchangeable with other components of the same type. This simple idea has three major implications. First, there is no real need to build or minutely specify all these components from scratch; things that were once built to custom specifications no longer need to be. Second, there is even less need to get locked-in to long-term contractual arrangements with one supplier; you should be able to swap between trusted services relatively easily. The hosting provider for GOV.UK was changed on several occasions to get a cheaper service without any visitors to the site noticing. Third, with technology getting cheaper and smarter as Moore's Law continues to hold, increasingly complex components will become commoditised as time passes.

In the UK, GOV.UK came in for criticism from people who thought the team wrote too much bespoke code. It was argued that the GDS could have deployed more commodity technology rather than trying to build our own answers to well-understood problems. Some of that criticism was fair. Part of the reason for the GDS writing much of GOV.UK was that doing so offered a learning opportunity to many developers in a way that simply implementing commodity technology would not. Should the organisation have effectively chosen to spend more money on GOV.UK to improve the technical ability of the civil servants who built it? There is an argument on both sides. Either way, there are always trade-offs to be made between flexibility and capability, and between commodity and customisation.

For governments, adopting open standards can play a huge role in driving up the take-up of commodity technology. Heroic work by officials and experts in the UK government helped break our bureaucracy's default dependency to expensive, proprietary technology choices. This saved money and helped thaw out a frozen government technology market. Having spent decades making contracting choices largely based on the supplier's name and ability to deliver things on a huge, lumbering scale, open standards made the government's technology buying decisions more about how to ensure flexibility and provide scale when it is needed, rather than going big from the very beginning. A change in philosophy like this doesn't create success overnight, but it does get an organisation to think much harder about technology in the context of its overall strategy – and it certainly wakes up the suppliers.

If the senior leadership of an organisation has little awareness of what is going on in the world of technology, they will be left to guess what to buy, build or hire, how much they should pay it, and what the strategic consequences of those choices might be. Too few executives ask to see the full wiring diagram for how their organisation's technology is set up. Being confronted with this horror is often reason enough for even the most incurious technophobe to wonder whether something might be amiss. Wardley mapping offers an excellent toolbox for helping those managers develop greater situational awareness,[46] but getting to that point requires an certain openness at an executive level to listening. It also means hiring technologists who know when to code, and when not to code, in positions that have a voice in making strategic decisions.

Wrangling people

Most large organisations have set themselves up to bring in the same sort of people on an industrial scale. This partly happens out of necessity; as people change jobs or leave, ready-made replacements have to be ready to step into the breach. That is fair enough, but as an unintended consequence, it also logically dictates the creation of standard, template recruitment processes and rules. There's a reason why big companies call the departments who run these systems 'human resources' – the philosophy sitting behind it is that the people are largely exchangeable, and easily replaced by others with similar skills and backgrounds. This undermines an organisation's diversity of appearance and diversity of mind.

Trying to transform a large organisation is therefore pretty much impossible without disrupting the norms applied to hiring people. When the GDS was starting out, the way government officials were hired in Britain was very similar in nearly every case. Applicants filled out a long form, writing lengthy answers to provide evidence and experience against certain competencies. If they passed this stage, they would be invited for an interview, where they will again be asked to articulate evidence for meeting a particular competency. This spiel didn't need to be any different from what they said on the form – candidates could sit and read it out loud, if they so wished. If their answers proved the most convincing, they were in. This process is clearly biased towards certain kinds of people. It works especially strongly against people who aren't strong writers or plausible when sitting in front of interrogative committees.

Digital teams need to bring in skills that can't be tested through this kind of process, or indeed, any single process. You can't draft your way to proving yourself a great designer or coder. Nor can a non-technical interviewer make a reasoned assessment about whether a technical architect is well qualified or not. Being able to change the typical way an organisation assesses applicants' employability and adapting the recruitment method for different types of skills are essential parts of a digital mandate.

The hacking of HR shouldn't stop after getting people through the front door. To build a digital institution capable of transforming the wider organisation you will have to break the other shackles that keep an organisation from hiring in its own image. That means looking at pay and introducing more options within the standard balance of rewards (not everyone will value a good pension or longer holidays over having more cash, for example). It means reviewing performance management systems that have few options for recognising excellence in career paths not expected to scale the senior leadership ladder. It means breaking grade structures that are designed to signpost the upward trajectory for a certain mixture of skills, and create perverse and dead-end promotions for specialists. The old trick of promoting the specialist into a management role, used as a last resort when it is the only way to pay specialists enough to stay, often lands those experts with responsibilities they don't want and are ill-qualified to handle.

The digital team's mandate must include permission to bend and test HR rules. This doesn't mean building a bonfire of procedures and process, no matter how tempting that might seem. Many of the existing principles that govern how an organisation handles its people will be perfectly sensible, but interpreted into uselessness by HR staff who lack any empowerment to take sensible and proportionate risks.

The quid pro quo for giving the digital team freedom to find better ways of hiring and looking after its people is that it must share the benefits of a better way with everyone else. There shouldn't be special dispensations for digital. If the digital team comes up with better job descriptions, innovative interview methods, or a more flexible pay framework, everyone else should share in the benefit.

Wrangling money

How an organisation chooses to invest money is a good test of its health and personality. In bureaucracies, especially those of a certain age, the business case process designed to appraise investments generally manages to pull off the worst of both worlds – it is both slow and arbitrary. Slow, because following the rules laid down by finance and procurement teams to the letter is a task that necessitates multiple people, several months and many thousands of largely redundant words. Some people view the time it takes bureaucracies to ruminate over investments as a source of strength. It combats hastiness, and allows the supporting logic for doing something to mature like a good wine. Unfortunately, in the majority of cases, the maturing process more closely resembles the effect time has on a good peach.

Lengthy business case processes add delay without adding more certainty. As a consequence, they fail to protect organisations from making poor choices. This is where the arbitrariness creeps back in. When confronted with a default route to getting things done that lasts longer than their likely term in post, legitimately impatient ministers or chief executives will simply resort to shouting loudly or conducting back-room favour exchanges to get what they want, without any recourse to analysis at all.

The traditional business case process typically applied by governments and large organisations is a neat example of a one-size-fits-all process that only properly serves a certain kind of project. This does not mean that it is useless. Through standardising certain processes, many governments have got much better at delivering certain kinds of project on time and within budget. Let's say a department is trying to build a large piece of infrastructure in a relatively controlled environment – a major new highway tunnel, for example. This is a well-understood problem, tackled in various forms before. The materials, behaviours and challenges at play are largely well-known. No major innovations or social changes are expected to dramatically alter the need for a tunnel. In this case, doing lots of upfront thinking in preparation for releasing one substantial chunk of money to get the work done is sensible.

Some tasks that governments and large organisations take on do occur within these relatively controlled environments. A great many do not. It is in these cases that the templates fall apart. The logic of being able to predict how future investments will turn out does not apply to projects and programmes with a large technology component. The market for new technology moves too fast for the business case process, as does the digital society in which the new policy or service is supposed to flourish. User expectations of what is possible, or even what is expected as a basic level of functionality, are accelerating all the time. Spend two years economically justifying all the requirements you demand of your new employee communications system, for example, and you'll find the world has changed in the meantime. This is why organisations end up being forced to defend the idea that in 2017 pagers are a perfectly good way of meeting your employees' communication needs.[47]

Creating a cumbersome process for releasing even small amounts of money is not a good use of time or brainpower, and reflects a very bureaucratic belief that terror of risk can be made to go away provided one simply writes everything down. If it takes you a year to write a business case, you want the investment it supports to last a lot longer than that – five or ten years, at least. Again, this is not a motivation well suited to the rapidly evolving world of digital technology. Nobody has a 10-year mobile phone contract. There's a reason for that.

Fixing the choice architecture for how money is spent in large organisations is no small task, especially those under the heavy scrutiny experienced by governments. The battle to win as a digital team is two-fold. You need a process that allows digital delivery teams to spend small amounts of money, quickly, in exchange for those teams demonstrating that the cash they've been given has allowed them to reduce the risk of scaling up their service for more people to use. Spending £50,000 to find out in four weeks if any of your 20 trial users will use a mobile app to log their weekly sugar intake is a lot safer than spending £10 million over two years on building an app, launching it to the world, and crossing your fingers. Traditional business cases push teams to gamble on the latter; if you have to write 200 pages of nonsense either way, why not go big?

Another, more insidious problem some very big organisations suffer from is the need to choose options that are reassuringly expensive. Large organisations have grown so used to receiving huge bills for their IT systems they cannot take the dramatically lower costs of commoditised technology seriously.

Money wrangles kill off many digital teams, because most processes for getting the money needed to get started on redesigning services either take too far long or are unable to release a small enough amount of money. Worse, they insist on teams being able to deliver many pages of fiction about how certain they are about the assumptions they make for their project's success. The truth is that many finance ministries or heads of finance would prefer to see a complete lie about the lifetime cost of a project than a relatively certain estimate of how much the next three months will cost – that is what their spreadsheet demands. This is cognitive dissonance operating on a grand scale.

Unpicking all of this will take a long time. In the UK, it took more than a year to put in place a business case process more suited to agile projects than the Treasury's waterfall-friendly Green Book guidance. As a digital team, your focus – beyond challenging and adapting default processes to stop them from breaking agile projects before they begin – is to help make sure that the people making investment decisions in your finance ministry or elsewhere are properly qualified to opine about technology. At the centre of most finance departments in government around the world is a cadre of young, intelligent and gifted amateurs. They know little or nothing about the area of spending they oversee, but they know the spending process inside out. Getting some people with internet-era technology knowledge, rather than good, generalist guessers, can completely transform the ability of a large organisation to invest wisely in technology-led change. A better process won't fix everything; you need different people too.

SUMMARY

- Digital institutions need a mandate that entitles them to influence processes and norms that apply across organisations.
- The digital team must avoid being lumped in with IT.
- The economic and strategic implications of using commodity technology and open standards are a significant part of what makes genuinely digital organisations viable.
- Challenging old HR processes is usually necessary to recruit scarce digital skills.
- Work with your finance department to create agile-friendly spending approvals.

Chapter 8

Reverting to type

Let's imagine the digital team you've set up has shipped some services to real people, and – by and large – they've gone down well. The rest of the business has begun to take notice. They might have won some public recognition, prizes even.[48] The team looks and sounds a bit different from everyone else. Nobody is exactly sure what it's going to do next.

For digital teams trying to change a big, lumbering organisation, there is a real advantage to keeping your strategic ambitions ambiguous for as long as possible. If people outside the team aren't precise about what you're trying to do or why, it makes it harder for them to reflexively object to what you're doing on principle. Any big organisational change will ruffle feathers. There will be plenty of people with a strong incentive to shut down the idea of a digital organisational change before any momentum can build, because it could make them look redundant, complacent or worse. It is harder for objections to wound if they come from a person who isn't sure what they're supposed to be violently opposed towards.

However, retaining this strategic ambiguity – which is just a slightly pretentious way of saying 'not writing your full plan down' – only works for as long as your digital team remains small. The outside world might not be completely sure what you're up to, but everyone within the circle needs to be crystal clear. Strategic ambiguity does not mean there is no plan. It means not explaining it in full until you're confident it's the right thing to do, preferably because you've delivered most of it already.

This is a controversial statement, but here it is: your plan should be based on reality. Most 5- or 10-year plans or digital strategies issued by companies or governments simply aren't. A long list of hopes and questionable assumptions is bundled together in an elegantly written paper drafted over the course of several months. No indication of the underlying uncertainty within the plan is given. This is then published. The document begins to degrade in usefulness from the minute it is finished. As and when reality intervenes, most organisations employ a sophisticated form of denial, where reality is bent around the plan. 'We met our targets,' they say. 'We may have changed how we measured those targets, but we definitely met them.' If things have gone really awry, the plan's very existence is forgotten entirely. There is no point in producing one of these documents. If you feel tempted to, that may be because the mix of skills in your team makes it incapable of doing anything else. The correct course of action here is to resist the urge and hire different people.

However, after a certain point, there are good reasons to sacrifice some strategic flexibility. The critical variable is scale. If your digital team has gone beyond the point where everyone knows everyone else by their first name – say 50–70 people – that may be a sign that it is time to introduce more clarity. Having an implicit plan to guide your work only succeeds when the networks of trust are small enough for the plan to be communicated to everyone without being lost in translation. In digital teams with around a hundred people or more, you need a more effective way of broadcasting and consulting on plans than corridor conversations.

The other variable is the sweep of influence the digital institution is seeking to exert over the organisation as a whole. In the first year or so, focusing on smaller services and building credibility can be done largely through personal relationships. Having won a licence to play on a bigger field, you will need some way of creating that credibility and trust at scale – and you can't personally meet and win over everybody. There's nothing for it. Now is the time to write a digital strategy.

What's my strategy?

Your digital strategy is not a shopping list of things for your current organisation to do. Implicitly or explicitly, it should be a recognition that your business or government has to become a different kind of organisation, a digital organisation. This will happen whether or not it wants to change. It is dealing with new types of problem, things that are unpredictable, undefined and constantly changing.[49]

The digital strategy must act as a signal towards the operating model you want your whole organisation to adopt and the culture that will allow that to happen successfully. While the content should focus on the practical steps that will help everyone on the way, the thread running through it is institutional change. This will come as a surprise to people who thought your job was fixing websites.

There are multiple routes to institutional change, from starting internally, to buying disruptors, to even quietly creating your own most feared competitor in a way that is semi-detached from your main business. One of your early strategic decisions is deciding which of these paths will not work best for your organisation, and therefore narrowing down your options.

Typically, writing a strategy is the first step that a team in government takes, long before anyone has tried delivering anything. The conclusions these documents draw therefore tend to come from abstract sources; literature reviews, international comparisons and economic models. All of these are valid foundations for basing important choices on, but they are only ever a partial reflection of reality – particularly for addressing anything involving a large measure of unpredictable human behaviour. The great advantage that a digital team will have is that, by the time you sit down to document your strategy for the next three to five years, you will already have an evidence base that offers a richer view than the usual sources. Data and user feedback on real services are a powerful complement to the traditional options from the strategy toolbox. Having a wider sweep of evidence to draw upon makes a digital strategy far more resilient to shifting circumstances than a standard strategy paper.

The trick for a good digital strategy is not to throw away orthodox techniques. A digital approach should add different (and sometimes competing) perspectives. Deploying different forms of evidence to work out problems and solutions – user research and web analytics taken from live services and prototypes, for example – gives you multiple bites at testing your assumptions, from different angles. You still might end up in the wrong place of course – no strategist can see into the future – but at least you will get a better idea of where your thinking is shakiest, and therefore needs more testing. The strategy really is delivery.

Taking a rounded view is the best way to write a digital strategy – any strategy really – that's worth having. Even

TRUST.
USERS.
DELIVERY.

A short, simple mission.
(Designed by Chris Thorpe.)

Digital government isn't just a big
story for the technology press.

The short countdown to launching GOV.UK.

Civil servants from GDS and beyond picking up
the 2013 Design of the Year award.
(Photo by the Design Museum.)

Royal crest, found in a London flea market.
Old design inspiring the new.

find
what
works

User research isn't about finding out what users like, but what works best for them.

not
what's
popular

Bringing disciplined user research into government made user-centred services possible.
(Written by Ella Fitzsimmons, designed by Mark Hurrell, illustration by Wil Freeborn.)

Kathy Settle and Neil Williams; the exemplary
bureaucratic hacker and digital deliverer.

GDS mission patches, created after a team had delivered
a public facing service. Linking culture to delivery.

The idea for mission patches came from a trip to the
Lyndon B. Johnson Space Center in Houston.

It's ok to...
say "I don't know"
ask for more clarity
stay at home when you feel ill
say you don't understand
ask what acronyms stand for
ask why, and why not
forget things
introduce yourself
depend on the team
ask for help
not know everything
have quiet days
have loud days, to talk, joke and laugh
put your headphones on
say "No" when you're too busy
make mistakes
sing
sigh
not check your email out of hours
not check your email constantly during hours
just Slack it
walk over and ask someone face-to-face
go somewhere else to concentrate
offer feedback on other people's work
challenge things you're not comfortable with
say yes when anyone does a coffee run
prefer tea
snack
have a messy desk
have a tidy desk
work how you like to work
ask the management to fix it
have off-days
have days off

Good working culture goes viral. GDS's 'It's OK...'
poster was passed around the world.
(Poster by Sonia Turcotte and Giles Turnbull,
photo by Graham Higgins.)

Words are the service. Content design was
a critical part of GOV.UK's success.
(Written by Sarah Richards, designed by Mark Hurrell.)

starting from this point, you still have to be careful. Most well intentioned and thought through strategy documents, corporate or government, end up gathering dust. You don't have time to waste on producing something that nobody reads. There are a few ways to avoid that fate.

Short and clear

Government officials are especially guilty of judging the quality of a strategy by its weight. There is a school of thought that believes that if you haven't exhaustively shown your working and bored an audience into limp submission, your output cannot be taken seriously. In its most extreme form, this extends to the vocabulary; if you haven't sprinkled the text with big words or business guff, you're apparently not smart enough to have big ideas.

Most of the time, the reverse is true. Your digital strategy should be concise. It should also be pleasurable to read, insofar as a strategy document ever can be. Writing a short, clear strategy is not purely for the readers' benefit. It exerts discipline on your thinking. If you are unable to express why you are making certain choices without resorting to long-winded officialese, the problem is as likely to be with the quality of the thinking as with the quality of the writing. If you don't understand what you've written, there's no chance anyone else will.

A good trick for keeping yourself honest is incorporating more than written words into the strategy. Include diagrams and short videos. Unlearning bad writing habits formed during years in a large corporate environment is not easy. Taking away the simple option of writing more words forces people to think more creatively, and stumble over the ambiguities that don't always make it through to the page. Apply the same tests to your visual language as your words. If a reader doesn't get the message you want to convey from a diagram first time, unprompted, the problem is with your diagram, not the reader, no matter how pretty your pictograms are.

Of the web, not on the web

The vast majority of government and corporate strategies are published as pdf documents, dumped on the web for later downloading. There are many good things about pdfs, but they are a bad format for anything that is a living document, rather than what the organisation reckons at a point in time. A digital strategy should be a website, not a pdf.

Publishing your strategy as a digital product is a good idea for the look of it; you're a digital team after all. A web native answer gives you more scope to move beyond text and incorporate other media, hyperlinks and reference material more neatly (it also makes it easier to add gimmicks and distractions, so be careful). However, the real benefit is that publishing web pages sets an expectation that this strategy is something that you will curate and update over time, as you learn more about the variables that will affect it.

A digital strategy should have the humility to say: 'We don't know what the future looks like. We do know unanticipated events will occur.' Rather than ignore this, as the typical static strategy document would do, pretending there is false certainty (and maintaining this illusion right up until the point when it's decided an entirely new strategy document is needed), a web strategy can embrace it. That's not an excuse to change the strategy whenever it's convenient or to conceal embarrassment. The version control on the website should make it very easy for readers to know where, when and why you have made any edits.

An incidental benefit that the GDS discovered during their work on the Government Digital Strategy in 2012 was that creating the strategy as a digital product provided an opportunity for the bureaucratic hackers usually involved in writing such things to get some experience of digital delivery. They learned Markdown, found their way around Github, set up stand-up meetings and a backlog. Producing your strategy as a digital product is a neat way of offering some role reversal opportunities within the digital team; the bureaucratic hackers get to do some rapid, iterative delivery, and the digital product teams create the conditions that allow them to get on with it. It also proves that even one of the most familiar artefacts of big organisations – the strategy paper – can be built digitally, in a simpler, faster way.

RETROSPECTIVE: CHALLENGER BANKS

Digitally skilled people often join large organisations with some expectation that they will invest time teaching their colleagues new tricks. In government, introducing policy wonks to code through drafting a digital strategy on the web is a neat example.

However, knowledge transfer is a process that should go both ways. In new banks challenging the industry's status quo (such as Monzo in the UK), teams have invested significant time in making sure their coders and designers understand the technicalities of banking, as much as they are helping the bankers get a grip on digital.

Challenger banks often run internal training on banking for their web engineers for this purpose. Investing this time gives those bringing new skills into an organisation more context about the situation they now find themselves in. It

> also makes clearer which rules, regulations and responsibilities cannot be ignored in the interest of innovation.
>
> For a balanced multidisciplinary team to work well, both the digital and bureaucratic experts need to recognise they have an obligation to spend some time learning more about the other.

Actions, not words

Flick through a typical strategy document, and you will often be impressed – awed, even – by the intricacies of logic and articulacy of argument within. Yet on reaching the end, you may feel a sense of emptiness. You go back through the document; there are justifications, targets, sweeping conclusions. Something is missing. 'That all sounds splendid,' you think, 'but what are you actually going to do?' We have seen – on several occasions – government strategies on topics from energy to healthcare where hundreds of pages of prose have been finished before, at the very end of the process, a few random actions or a half-hearted delivery plan are squeezed in at the last minute. The chapter structure of these documents is revealing. Usually, they are organised by topic or policy area. These exercises are about what we are, not what we do.

A digital strategy should reject this. For the digital team, what you are is what you do. The lion's share of your short digital strategy should be devoted to explaining what you plan to deliver, when you'll have it done by, and who is responsible for getting it finished.

One of the debates you will need to have as you agree these actions is about deadlines. One of the cards a good digital team can play is that it is able to get things started quickly. That is not the same as saying that it is always going to get a service fully live and operational more quickly than what has happened before. This is a subtle difference, but an important one. Putting deadlines against your actions is not a bad idea; it focuses teams, keeps momentum high and provides natural points to review whether the overall strategy is still the right one. The skill is setting the right expectation about what will be delivered by that deadline – a minimum viable product used by 25 people, a fully working service in front of millions of users, or something in between. If you don't know, opt to under promise and over deliver; it is better to have a disagreement than a nasty surprise.

Organisational context

There is a good chance that while you're writing your digital strategy, several other teams in the organisation will be setting out their own grand plans. There will also probably be other existing strategies that your efforts must at least be seen to coincide with.

In the UK, the Government Digital Strategy was published at the same time as plans for civil service reform, national broadband rollout and, most importantly, a programme of widespread austerity in response to the 2008 financial crisis. All of these would have been government priorities with or without the digital strategy supporting them. The digital strategy was an opportunity to reinforce the aims of each individual plan, as well as presenting a degree of strategic coherence from the organisation as a whole.

The political or corporate context inevitably informs the tone and emphasis of a digital strategy, but it shouldn't define all the content. In the UK, if the economic times had been more rosy, the potential savings arising from moving services online would have been less in the spotlight. If civil service reform hadn't been a clear objective of the government (and owned by the same minister who was responsible for the digital agenda), the digital strategy may not have been so explicit about claiming a mandate for institutional and leadership change. But in any version of the political atmosphere, the actions that a workable digital strategy needs to include are roughly the same. Context frames the problems to be solved; it doesn't explain how to solve them. That plan needs to come from you.

Giving others the opportunity to take some credit for your plan is rarely a bad idea in a big organisations, and making sure your strategy contributes to others is a smart bet. Only do this when the mutual objectives really do coincide, however. The worst thing to do is to allow your digital strategy to become a document trying to capture all the organisation's IT moans and technophilia in one place. You need a workable plan, not a shopping list.

Getting agreement

Of course, writing a strategy down is only one piece of the puzzle. The real challenge is getting people to agree to it.

Getting agreement to a digital strategy is really no different to getting agreement to anything else in a large organisation or bureaucracy. It takes patience, a deep knowledge of the protocols, and no small amount of cunning. This is where your bureaucratic hackers will step in.

With any luck, the digital team will have begun to win some friends by aligning with other plans. These other strategies will have their objectors, however, so you may acquire those critics too, as well as your own personal detractors.

There will still be plenty of people in your organisation who will equate digital with IT, or possibly with social media and communications. Many of those will therefore view your work as too technical, involved and dull for them to trouble themselves with. It can be tempting to just let this indifference lie, concentrating instead on those who show some interest. Starting with the enthusiasts is a good idea for building support; the more powerful cheerleaders you have around the organisation advocating on your behalf, the less glad-handing you need to do personally. You should resist the impulse to focus only on friendly faces though, because it is the unengaged who will cause the problems later. Do not pretend that a digital strategy is anything other than a plan to transform how the whole organisation goes about delivery, and therefore something that will affect them. It's better for them to find out now.

Getting agreement to the strategy is one of those tasks where it usually makes sense for the digital team to follow recognised organisational patterns rather than try and develop some new, disruptive path to agreement. Now is not the time to come out all guns blazing to change the standard business case format, say, however unhelpful it may be. Before you get the chance to change the game, you first have to prove you understand the rules. Following procedures now also offers some protection for later. When the going gets tough, you want there to be absolutely no doubt that the direction of travel you've set out was indeed ratified by everyone who should have ratified it, and look, here's the piece of paper that confirms it.

For us in the UK, this meant getting sign-off to the digital strategy from a Cabinet Committee; a group of senior ministers representing all of Whitehall's biggest fiefdoms. The meeting itself is largely a formality, of course – the real work takes place in the discussions, write rounds and phone calls beforehand. As the process of 'stakeholder handling' drags on, there may be a temptation to circumvent particularly tricky people by going straight to their boss or minister. This is a tactical call that you may end up regretting, especially in government. A minister may disappear in 18 months; an official can hate you forever.

Along the way to building some consensus behind the strategy, you will have to make some compromises. Making your first draft very ambitious is never a bad idea, as it gives you more chips to bargain with later. Some compromises are better than others. Compromises that involve extending deadlines, widening financial targets, or taking out actions you're not certain are correct are the best concessions. They allow you to admit that there is still lots of uncertainty, but maintain that the basic strategic premise of institutional reform is right. Compromises that substitute clear actions for mealy-mouthed language, let individual departments off the hook or excuse poor performance indefinitely are not a good idea, and you should fight against them.

SUMMARY

- Your strategy should reflect what you have learned through delivering; don't rely on assumptions or presentation of false certainties.
- Focus on agreeing small, time-bound actions, and admit uncertainty where it exists.
- A digital strategy must be of the web and on the web. Think in web pages, not paper.

- Make the effort to engage the unengaged, as delaying this will create problems later.
- Use the strategy to give others support or cover for positive things they are trying to do in their own department.

Chapter 9

Running the numbers

How many services do you, as an entire organisation or central government, offer to users or to citizens and businesses? Take a guess. Fifty? A couple of hundred? Several thousand? You probably don't know. That's forgivable. No one else in your organisation knows either.

As the digital team is starting to spread its wings and build up a reputation for delivery far beyond its four walls, thoughts will turn to the bigger, thornier service design challenges it can get its teeth into. It is time to look at fixing some of the bigger transactions on the books, the brownfield services your organisation or government has long laboured over, where there are unimpressed users and savings to be made. To make a start on that, you need to know where to prioritise.

Finding out which of your organisation's services are the most used can be a surprisingly difficult question to answer. For a government, even if you take out the multitude of services which are offered at a local or state level, there are still many separate public bodies to explore. Systematically working out which services are the most broken from a user's perspective can be even harder, short of relying on anecdotes and horror stories. Gathering basic data on services should be one of the team's first deep forays into the numbers behind digital transformation.

Exploring transactions

In the months leading up to writing your digital strategy you may feel the sense that nobody is quite clear on exactly how big a challenge the process of transforming your organisation will be, at least not in cold, hard numbers. The GDS committed itself to making making all new or redesigned government services handling more than 100,000 transactions a year 'digital by default'. That sounds like a very lofty ambition, but how difficult is that exactly? How many services does central government offer that are that big? Nobody knew. This was mostly because nobody in a central position had bothered to ask. Delivery was not something the centre had concerned itself with before; if departments wanted to collect the data, that was their lookout. Creating a full service catalogue – essentially, a very big list – was the first step towards putting in place data that enables a digital team to plan for a successful digital transformation at scale.

The GDS's version of this catalogue was called the Transactions Explorer. In its earliest versions, the Explorer was not a particularly sophisticated thing. It started life as a spreadsheet with three columns: the name of a service, the department that ran it, and how many transactions it handled each year. The information was gathered via requests from each individual department, sent out once per quarter. The collated version was then published for the world to see. Over time, the Explorer would add detail for other indicators, like cost per transaction, and evolve into a published, real-time performance dashboard for government services.

While much of this data will be familiar to operational staff, many people operating at the policy or strategy level of an organisation – those making decisions that directly affect users and the frontline staff who actually see them – are rarely confronted with this basic service information. This is one of the effects of splitting organisations into separate silos rather than mixing them into multidisciplinary teams. For staff operating at a policy level, frontline delivery metrics are someone else's problem to worry about.

Numbers without behaviour distortion

Admitting there are imperfections in any quantitative measurement is generally a wise position to adopt in government. Government data tends to be treated with hushed respect, as if it was unimpeachably accurate. The standards that most democratic governments set themselves in terms of data quality are rightly high, and nation states generate more reliable numbers than most other sources. That does not mean they offer perfection. Even now, at the beginning of almost every official data-gathering exercise is a fallible human being with a spreadsheet to fill in.

Taking a qualified view of your organisation's numbers leads to another important change in the team's attitude towards data: trust the trend line more than than the exact number. While the numbers are probably not too bad, there's no guarantee you can rely on them for making fair comparisons. However many guidelines, definitions and demands you set, for as long as data is gathered by humans in bureaucracies, different departments will report on the same numbers in different ways.

One thing you should therefore avoid looking for in your service catalogue is winners and losers, or creating league tables comparing different services. The data won't be reliable enough, and the services not similar enough to do this fairly. Only the most blatantly broken or brilliant services will stand out from their peers, and you probably know those already. Rather than forcing false comparisons between different things that might give a false picture, pick the most likely point of consistency – reports that come from the same department about the same service – and pay attention to those. The trend line from a reliable source of data offers an indicator of relative progress or decline. The more dependable data sources are brought together, the better position a digital team will be in to spot issues.

The UK government's transaction data contained a couple of insights that prove common in most large organisations. No matter how many services an institution is running, as a general rule the vast majority of transactions take place in a relatively small number of them – the top 10% in terms of volume typically account for 90% of all the transactions taking place across the whole of government. The rest make up the 'long tail'. Quite a lot of these will be very small indeed. The UK's environment department receives around 10 applications a year for burials at sea, for example. For the digital team, prioritising how best to achieve the strategic ambitions for digitisation suddenly becomes more straightforward. Fix the top 10% of services, and you can deliver the vast majority of benefit to users.

Another less obvious conclusion from the GDS's performance dashboards was the realisation of just how terrible the organisation had become at naming services. When you look at services one by one, it is easy to forget how cryptic their function must be to somebody who is unfamiliar with it. When confronted with a list of 700 or more services all described as word jumbles, you begin to realise how often services are named for the benefit of government or business, to the confusion of users. The names are also a pretty good indicator for how much the service as a whole was designed with users in mind. The GDS's head of service design, Louise Downe, provided a good rule of thumb: 'Good services are verbs, bad services are nouns.'[50]

By far the most important insight from digging into the data, however, was the power of transparency.

Make things open, it makes things better

There was a lot of nervousness about publishing the Transactions Explorer. Instinctively, when most public officials think of publication they consider the risks this entails, rather than the benefits. As a government's default position is to retain information, and the personal rewards for officials deviating from that default are scant, their bias is to only see problems in openness. From an individual perspective, that's fair enough. From a whole of government view, it is harder to defend. The public paid for that data. Unless it imperils national security, there's a good case for them having access to it.

Governments around the world have spent a good deal of energy in recent years developing performance league tables looking at various arms of the state – schools, surgeries, and so on. This work is generally badged as 'deliverology': the process of establishing a small team focused on performance, gathering performance data to set targets and trajectories, and having routines to drive and ensure a focus on performance.[51] Much of it is sensible, basic project management, rarely a bad idea for governments to stick with. The performance tables are also supposed to support the idea of greater choice in public services (something which in practice doesn't always happen very much). In either case, the psychology behind them is clear; there is a strong incentive for the low performers to avoid the embarrassment of a lowly position, and for the high performers to aspire for the top spots.

Publishing the Transactions Explorer in the open effectively turned this psychological trick back on the officials who had been happily deploying it on their public sector colleagues for years. If a department failed to submit their data to the Transactions Explorer, they wouldn't be left off the public list. Instead, in their place would be the blank space their numbers should have occupied. In time, as more of those blank spaces were filled, the remaining voids began to look more shameful for the departments and agencies unable or unwilling to divulge the data.

As an open data set, the Transactions Explorer wasn't especially interesting. It wasn't big enough to be suited to data mining, nor was it controversial enough to interest journalists. The value of transparency in this case was to change the incentives acting on civil servants. Failing to publish data made you look bad professionally, the reverse of what was typically the case.

Measuring performance

The Transactions Explorer began as a simple measure of transaction volume. This information was necessary to work out where it made sense to prioritise digital team's efforts for delivering the biggest impact. Simply going after the most widely used services wasn't a particularly nuanced strategy, however. The largest transaction handled by the UK government was Stamp Duty Reserve Tax: payments made on share purchases. It handles over a billion transactions a year, but is an automated process and not public-facing – not a sensible candidate for transformation. So as well as needing to refine how it would choose projects to work on, the GDS also needed to give teams building digital services all over government a clear answer about what measures mattered.

Measuring organisational performance is a sprawling, many-sided debate. There are as many perspectives on the 'right' things to measure as there are 'right' ways to measure them. Some businesses measure hundreds of different variables in their quest for profitability. Most governments tend to be similarly thorough, with the added complication of managing multiple desired outcomes at the same time, where the operational measures often fail to match up with lofty political goals.

In the UK, to keep things simple, we selected four performance metrics: digital take-up, completion rate, cost per transaction and user satisfaction. We could have picked more. Four was a manageable number, and effectively covered the bases for the GDS's primary strategic aims: getting more people to use online government services, building services that worked first time, saving money and meeting user needs.

As soon as you set performance indicators and determine a baseline for how things look before you've tried to improve the picture, you will be strongly encouraged to set a target number: a goal that you will strive to hit by a certain point in time. Be very careful about this.

Targets are a controversial topic in government circles. For some, they are simple and cheap way of pointing a complicated entity in one direction. To others, they are blunt tools, responsible for creating perverse incentives and questionable outcomes. The truth is probably somewhere between the two. Targets have undoubtedly helped drive improved performance in some specific areas. They tend to be especially good in fields where direct comparisons are relatively straightforward and there is a low chance for human beings to game the system by focusing on meeting the target rather than the intent lying behind it. But where the scope for variation and gaming is high, problems arise.

Let's take digital take-up as an example. The GDS could have set itself a target for 80% online take-up for all of the UK government's digital services. Approximately four-fifths of the UK population was online in 2012 – 80% sounds like a reasonable if ambitious target. Dig a little deeper though, and things begin to unravel. For some services, such as registering to vote, the simplicity of the transaction and nature of the people likely to use it means that aiming for a target nearer 95% might be more reasonable. Applying for certain forms of benefit is, on the other hand, a far more involved process with a very different set of users. In that case, reaching 70% digital take-up represents a significant achievement. As a specific target, 80% manages to be wrong in both directions. So would any other number. If you were to avoid setting individual service targets and instead take 80% digital take-up as an aggregate aim across all government services, there would be a strong argument for the digital team and departments to focus their efforts on services that offered the simplest processes and most digitally confident users just to make the numbers add up.

That kind of gaming doesn't reflect a particularly cynical or nefarious view of government officials – it is just what rational actors would do. Not all officials would agree with focusing on the easy service as a fair strategy, which would lead to internal arguments, which in turn would lead to delays. Exactly the same problems can be imagined from gaming cost per transaction targets, completion rates or user satisfaction. None of this benefits users.

If targets are too tempting to ignore altogether, they should be set on a service-by-service basis, and relative to a baseline: to cut the cost of issuing a fishing licence by a third, or increase completion rates of self-assessment tax forms by 10%, for example.

While avoiding targets was the right decision, we didn't get all of our metrics right. User satisfaction proved perennially difficult to draw conclusions from, no matter how it was measured. The problem with user satisfaction was finding numbers that could give a reliable indication of relevant information to measure performance or improve a service. Was the service meeting user needs? For businesses, this is a little more straightforward; if a user is not satisfied, they can look elsewhere. The problem for governments everywhere is that their digital service can meet user needs very successfully while still leaving the user dissatisfied. It is a rare person who concludes the process of paying the government their taxes by leaving a thank you message for the smoothness of the experience.

In government, measuring user satisfaction picks up false signals: about how happy people are about paying tax, even about how happy they are with the government's political performance in general. These are not things that any digital service team can do anything about. In the end, the most reliable way to measure user satisfaction was in the research lab, watching real people use the service. This was difficult to scale, but always worth the effort.

The GDS's choice of four performance metrics acted as useful pointers for stories to celebrate or worries to address. They weren't designed to provide the people managing the services day to day with all the detailed insight needed to make incremental improvements to services; more detailed web analytics packages delivered that. What they offered was an indication of relative progress, and a measure of momentum.

Money

While putting an accurate figure on user satisfaction can prove almost impossible, one metric can not be ignored entirely. Making a compelling argument that shows digital transformation can save money or generate revenue is crucial in persuading your organisation to take a step into the unknown. For the UK government between 2010 and 2015, austerity was the biggest game in town. It is no exaggeration to say that the economic conditions and resultant squeeze on public finances was the single biggest factor emboldening the digital agenda in government. Without it, making the political case for institutional reform would have been a much bigger challenge; good times make defending the bureaucratic status quo a much more straightforward task.

In the Digital Efficiency report published at the same time as the Government Digital Strategy, the GDS made an economic case for digital transformation. The report showed that taking a digital by default approach to government services could save the government £1.8 billion over the course of the parliament, and eventually reduce the government's cost by almost £2 billion a year.[52]

Constructing economic arguments for digital services is more of an art than a science. There is now plenty of circumstantial evidence to draw on from other institutions, and lots of examples detailing the relative costs of using phone, post, face-to-face and digital channels to carry out a particular service. Even with this, constructing a case for an analogue government or business to adopt digital is not straightforward. If an organisation has never tried something like this before, there are few direct precedents or data points for them to build an argument upon.

There are three main benefits to building economic arguments for digital transformation. It proved that the digital team took the financial case for digitisation seriously enough to conduct a detailed piece of analysis, which meant that analytically inclined officials were more minded to trust the team's intentions than they would have otherwise been. Second, the report gave an indication of the savings that were possible, setting an appropriate level of expectation. While exact figures wouldn't be perfect, it set an order of magnitude for the potential prize. Digital wasn't pocket change to government – even in the zeros-filled world of government accounting, 10-figure amounts are worthy of notice. Digital transformation could therefore be positioned as a substantial side-dish within the government's overall savings menu, but not as a main course.

The third, and somewhat accidental, benefit to publishing an economic case for digitisation was that it allowed the GDS to avoid setting itself a hard target for making savings. The £1.8 billion figure for savings by 2015 set an expectation. Nonetheless, it was not a formal target. This meant that the digital team didn't have to organise its behaviour and priorities around financial targets in the way a unit solely dedicated to saving money would. This provided a small but crucial difference in outlook. The digital institution could keep a focus on meeting user needs at the same time as saving government money. If these priorities had been reversed – saving money before meeting needs – it is unlikely the users would get much of a look in.

SUMMARY

- Write a list of all the services your organisation provides and use it to gauge where digital change can have the biggest impact for users.
- Choose performance metrics that give clues as to how well you are meeting user needs; these may differ from organisational objectives.
- Use metrics to judge velocity of change, rather than setting hard targets.
- Make an economic case for applying digital transformation to your organisation.
- Move away from spreadsheet data requests to automated real-time data collection as fast as you can.

Chapter 10

Consistent, not uniform

We must design for a fast changing world ... rather than
retreating to the sterility of traditional techniques and built-in
obsolescence. We need an aesthetic of change.

— Richard Rogers, *A Place for All People*

M ost large organisations possess a talent for dullness.
Governments raise this into a fine art. Announcements
from the corridors of power are carefully dried and stripped
of personality, making even the most interesting stories
seem bland.

In their more cynical moments, senior officials and ministers use the power of boredom to their advantage. It can obfuscate, confuse and ultimately bore people into not properly
holding them to account. Holding a government's side of the
story up to the light becomes test of stamina; if you have the
fortitude to trawl through the verbiage and jargon, the truth
may reveal itself.

This can be just as much of a problem for people working within the organisation as it is to those on the outside.
Those who are looking to improve what they're doing make
it easy for others to ask questions and give feedback. Few
large organisations and even fewer governments do this. This
is partly because those working in them are worried that they
won't be able to respond.

Most of the time, however, officials aren't deliberately setting out to tell stories tedious enough to move the focus of attention elsewhere. Governments and other large organisations usually have a neutral or positive message they want to convey. This problem is that most people working in them are unable to communicate this in the style we now expect, or are simply not allowed to.

Breaking through this barrier can be especially hard in government. Part of the job description for public officials in many countries is to stay in the shadows. The political layer tells the stories, constructing a narrative that fits their aims. An official's job is to press hard kernels of fact into their boss's hands, and encourage them to use those facts wisely and fairly. There are few incentives for sensible officials to put their own heads above the parapet – and many are expressly forbidden from doing so.

This approach to government communications is reflected in the structures put in place to manage them. Every government department – as with large corporate organisations – has a dedicated communications team. They handle relationships with journalists, monitor the media, fight fires and offer rebuttals, and try to secure favourable coverage wherever possible. Their main job, however, is to control what message the organisation puts out to the world.

This may sound like a strategic job, aimed at securing a long-term goal like the successful landing for an important government commitment. In fact, the reality is usually much more tactical. Unless things start going wrong earlier in the piece, a government communications team only gets involved at the end of a policymaking process. Their job is to try and translate some finalised technical policy language into words that normal people might understand, make sure it sounds coherent with everything else the department is doing (whether it is or not), put a ribbon and bow around the announcement, and find somewhere for the minister to stand up and read the speech she is handed by her policy team. Very little of this is communication, in the true sense of the word. It is message handling for the benefit of the news cycle. This artificial storytelling creates a gap between what you see on the news and what is really going on.

Telling different stories

One of the most powerful ways for a digital institution to differentiate itself from the rest of its organisation is to interact with the outside world in a different way. In practical terms, this boils down to four things: catchphrases, openness, internet-era tools, and making communications an integral part of delivery.

1. Catchphrases

Some phrases have the power to spread quickly. This can be seen in the memes and viral in-jokes of the internet, the pieces of online conversation that are so easily replicated and adapted they seem to appear everywhere, instantly. These ideas, behaviours or phrases can spread from person to person with immense efficiency. Small ideas, infinitely copyable.

We should be careful here. We're not saying – really not saying – that a digital team should spend its time emulating the production of viral cat videos and imagining that saying 'we're of the internet, this is what we do' to the rest of your organisation will go down well. People will, quite rightly, take this as their cue not to take you seriously.

Nevertheless, the principles that lie behind how to spread successful memes are instructive for any team trying to achieve widespread change. The biggest challenge facing any new digital team sat within a huge organisation – government or otherwise – is explaining what it is doing, how and why. To succeed, it must do this on a grand scale, leaving potentially hundreds of thousands of people with little ambiguity about the intentions you have. It must also be able do this at speed. Given how fast a digital team should be delivering and iterating on what it does, there is no point in your organisation or the outside world only understanding what you're up to 12 months after your strategy has pivoted to something else. Traditional methods of conveying a message of change across big organisations don't always offer that speed. Government is full of great writers that suit a broadcast style of messaging; these are the elegant constructors of the white paper and legislative amendment. Unfortunately, these logical, structured outputs aren't designed to transmit rapidly at scale – they are too complex, nuanced and complete. What's really needed to communicate big ideas at pace throughout a system isn't sublime prose. It's advertising.

Other than the digital strategy we wrote about in chapter 7, the GDS wrote and published very few things that roughly followed the format of a traditional government paper. Instead, the team focused on creating short phrases, blog posts and presentations that formed the basis of a different method for how civil servants could communicate, both with each other and the people they were working for.

Government communications tend to be trapped between an egotistical yet insecure view of themselves. On the one hand, public organisations firmly believe they are important institutions of substance and meaning. However, most public institutions know their power and influence is more transient that they would like to admit. This insecurity leads governments to wear all that substance on their sleeves, producing documents and press releases that make no effort to hide the intellect and effort that goes into them. The trick for a successful digital team comes in feeling confident enough in the substance of what it is delivering to tell the world about it in a way that invites a conversation, rather than an orchestrated round of applause.

For the GDS, this work included crafting what would later become familiar digital catchphrases, first in the UK and then around the world. 'Show the thing'; 'Simpler, clearer, faster'; 'Consistent, not uniform'; 'Make things open, it makes things better'; 'Start with user needs'; 'It's OK to...'; 'Digital by default'; 'The strategy is delivery'. Some of these went viral, for want of a better phrase, and some didn't. Flat on the page, these short phrases might seem obvious, facile even. But they were incredibly powerful because they were tied to the delivery of tangible things. A small number of short statements made it immediately obvious what the digital team was trying to do. Like a good jingle or slogan, people remembered them. Posters were printed out and stuck them on walls. Stickers displayed them on laptops. Slide presentations were full of them. The catchphrases also made pithily clear that a digital organisation represented something quite different; this was not the verbose, technical language of analogue government.

The logic of catchphrases also applied to naming things. Governments are terrible at naming things. Take 'V890 SORN', the name of a service that the UK central government provides. What's SORN? It's a Statutory Off Road Notification. OK. What's that? It's the form you have to fill in when you register your vehicle as no longer used on the road. Fine. Let's call it that then. The UK government now has a service called 'Register your vehicle as off the road'. Similarly, there's a prize for anyone who can guess what the 'IER' service does. If you guessed voter registration, congratulations; you can now participate in your democracy. The GDS didn't think passing an acronym quiz should be a prerequisite to voting, so we called the new digital service 'register to vote' instead.

Every step taken towards simplicity is another barrier removed for users. It's also a step closer to making things more straightforward for colleagues. Use language that works at scale. This is not about sloganeering or 'selling' a digital agenda internally, though it can undoubtedly have a rhetorical benefit. Writing and saying what you mean is fundamental to the vision lying behind products, services and organisational changes that a digital team should be trying to effect.

2. Openness

The default position for a digital team working anywhere – especially in government – should be to publish what it is up to. One of the GDS's first acts was to set up a blog for the team to explain their progress on building GOV.UK for all to see and comment on.

Blogging by big organisations often ends up being a strange mix of corporate messages and peeks into a bowdlerised version of a senior executive's diary: 'Last week I went on a wonderful site visit to see our hardworking staff in the Worksop office.' Real news is saved for press releases, and the senior executive's true opinions for the pub. If your organisation's blogs read like this, close them down immediately. Nobody is reading them.

There is also not much point in only making a tiny part of your communications open, and leaving most of it to a closed, controlled approach. A thin chink of transparency is tokenistic and lacks authenticity. Nobody will be fooled. Blogging and social media should not be thought of as an add-on to a traditional communications approach; it is there to largely replace it.

Openness needs to be the default mode of working across a digital team. The blog is where you put news, admit your mistakes and celebrate the team's successes. Once a digital team is up and running, it should be able to publish something new every few days. In the 5 weeks leading up to the launch of GOV.UK, the GDS published over 30 blog posts. If people want to know what's going on in the digital institution, be they colleague, journalist or interested member of the public, they go to the blog to find out. No more press releases.

This does not diminish the importance of digital teams in government building good relationships with journalists, nor the time and effort that requires. Many journalists have become used to getting the inside track on what the government is up to from their contacts. Some may feel irked by the amount of transparency in blogs because they are left playing catch up with everyone else rather than breaking stories themselves. Investing the time building relationships with journalists built on trust and reciprocity will pay dividends later, alerting you to risks and pitfalls before the team unwittingly stumbles into them. Others in your organisation will notice the benefits, and look to copy the digital team's methods. As Emer Coleman, the GDS's first Head of Communications, wrote in 2012, 'Many more of my government communication colleagues across Whitehall will begin to explore how different relationships can be built through the behaviours we manifest in the social web, and how ultimately that just might be a good thing for government.'

Openness is about what you say as much as where you say it. Having part of a large corporate or government talk candidly about what it is doing and what it plans to do next is still unusual. Having those same organisations openly and humbly admitting failings and missteps is radical. You should do as much of this as you can get away with. In the early days in particular, the GDS published a number of blog posts describing in some detail what the team had got wrong. We did less of this as time went on, and, in hindsight, that was a mistake.

Showing humility is a scary idea in most large organisations. Yet being able to candidly admit faults while explaining how you plan to fix them quickly is a demonstration of strength. The flexibility and agility of an effective digital team should make it easier for you to correct errors than other parts of your organisation. Showing a different way of reacting to failure sends a powerful message. When you genuinely aren't in control of the situation, conceding vulnerability rather than allowing the pressure to build up into a large and messy catastrophe is a good idea. Of course, this is easier said than done. Governments and large organisations have a huge bias towards crossing their fingers and hoping. Yet there is no shortage of examples where this has proved unwise.

3. Internet-era tools

A digital organisation will use the web to tell its stories.

Because the word 'digital' has become so bound up in some perceptions the world of marketing and communications, people outside the digital team may be expecting it to use all kinds of bleeding-edge social media tools to tell your story to the outside world. Those same people will find it oddly hilarious if a member of a digital team brings their paper notepad to a meeting. In both cases, the point is not about the technology – it is about selecting the best tool available for the task. A blog and a handful of social media accounts will get you most of the way.

A digital team should experiment with social media to see what works for its audience and ensure it is using the most effective channels for reaching them. A government team, especially, has a duty to figure out whether it is reaching a wide enough group of people. Try new things. The GDS staff tested Periscope for live video streaming. We tried using videos for the organisation's weeknotes rather than written blog posts. Staff jumped onto comment boards when questions on GOV.UK came up (two of the Office of National Statistics digital team did an official AMA session – ask me anything – on Reddit). Some of it worked, some of it didn't. Be as iterative with your approach to communicating as you are with the products you build.

The GDS began with one blog for the whole organisation and made that part of government communications infrastructure. From there, the team created many more tightly focused blogs, each with discrete and defined audiences, covering a huge variety of topics from user research to data science and HR. These created bounded spaces for experts to write to an audience they knew was interested, starting a conversation rather than a broadcast. They opened up networks, and left a legacy of knowledge that is still available for anyone to draw on. In many large organisations, hoarding information in emails and memos is a common form of controlling power. Publishing in the open breaks that model, and distributes power more widely. Wrangling with corporate communications teams is a time-consuming chore in all large organisations; using digital tools and practices is an easy way to hack around them. This annoys the hoarders, but is very much worth it.

4. Communications is part of delivery

One of the most important habits you will need to break as a digital team is the idea that communicating about delivery is the job of a communications specialist. Your digital institution will need a team dedicated to communications. They will own the channels you use, set expectations about the style, look and feel, and make sure there isn't a complete free-for-all. But they are the curators of how your institution communicates, not the creators. The teams delivering digital products and services are themselves responsible for telling the world what they are up to and how it is going.

This does not necessarily mean that each digital product team should have a communications specialist in it. Everyone on the team, be they developer, researcher, designer or manager, is expected to contribute to the flow of communication. This will not come naturally to everybody. To some, it will feel like a distraction from the 'real' business of getting things shipped. This response is worth challenging. While imposing the discipline needed to openly communicate about how a product is developing can feel like a distraction, it is an excellent indicator of the product's health. If you can't write clearly about what you're trying to do, or don't feel you can be honest in print about the challenges you face, then there are some bigger questions the team needs to face up to.

Part of the trick in making collective communication feel less of a burden is to reduce both the number of channels you use, and the amount of tailoring that is applied to the way the team communicates. Teams in large organisations tend to tell different stakeholders what's going on through individual meetings and emails, tailoring every message to their particular concerns, and doing so in fixed, irregular bursts. They send, rather than publish, what they are up to.

If the team correctly anticipates all these individual concerns correctly, this works fine. If they don't, and it is six months before the next round of 'consultation' is planned, you leave a confused or angry stakeholder stewing for a long time. Communicating little and often through the same open channel, and with the same message for internal and external stakeholders, makes you more flexible and responsive to questions.

One of the communication gaps for most large organisations is creating space for teams to express pride in the work they have done internally. Changing anything is hard. A lot of the time, teams going through that journey are left with little more than mental scars. To fill this gap, the GDS used stickers.

Early in 2012 two of the GDS team visited NASA in Houston. They saw the patches the astronauts designed for each mission and inspiration struck.

From then on, each GDS team was awarded a mission patch for delivering a public-facing, time-bound project. They designed it themselves, including the GDS motto 'TRUST, USERS, DELIVERY' and featuring an animal somewhere on the patch

All the patch design rules were broken. That didn't matter. Something as simple as a few stickers (which the teams paid for themselves) created very visible signs of progress, and a form of creative expression that was owned by the teams themselves. They put in the hard work to deliver something; they could then display that effort with pride. Allowing individuals to express themselves and feel ownership of the delivery stories they played a part in is a huge part of the culture behind successful transformation.

Presenting in real life

It is not enough to tell stories on the web. You will have ample opportunities to do it in real life too.

Anyone with professional experience in any office-based organisation, large or small, public or private, will at some point have come down with a bad case of PowerPoint poisoning. It begins with a feeling of disorientation, followed by heaviness in the limbs. Left untreated, it leads to depression.

The quality of presentations given around the world, even in the loftiest boardrooms by the most expensive consultants, is generally awful. Presenters are often caught between trying to say too much or having nothing at all to say. As a digital team, you should invest time, thought and effort in the way you present yourself. Too often, teams in big organisations do vast amounts of good work only to trip up at the end with confusing slides.

Being a good presenter does not mean being a charismatic, articulate extrovert (these can be the most self-indulgent presenters). It means doing the basics properly. Say what you actually think. Restrict yourself to a handful of words per slide, so it can be read from anywhere in the room. One idea per slide. Plan your story from end to end. Explain what this structure is to your audience before you dive in. Practicing beforehand. Keep it short – no one has ever complained about a talk being too short.

None of this is complicated, but it does require hard work. Like the rest of your communications, investing time in decent presentations should be part of delivery, not something rushed into at the end. Read www.doingpresentations.com for practical tips on good presenting, and especially the three blog posts on making presentations big, clear and bearable.

Designing for users

Good design is easy to understand. Like a joke, if you have to explain it, it's not that good.

Governments and big businesses are rarely mentioned in the same breath as good design. Over the last 30 years, the state machinery in most democratic nations has seemed largely uninterested in its power. In the place of design organisations have put advertising gloss and campaigning sophistry, when it can be afforded, there to drape a thin cloak over the rough cogs of policy and implementation.

The power of architecture, visual design, art and iconography has been undervalued by a generation of public officials who instinctively discount what cannot be fitted into a rigid business case assessment. Making things look good is seen as a luxury at best, and a distraction at worst.

This is unwise, because today's best services are very well designed. The most successful digital organisations invariably find a strong voice for design (Airbnb was famously started by two designers). Services offered by organisations that are not digital natives need to be well designed too. But to do that, they will have to go about design in an unfamiliar way.

Good design meets a clear user need. User needs are hard to identify. You find them by studying what people do, not what they say they do. A well-designed service does the hard work to make things simple. Simplicity is hard; demanding discipline, focus and sacrifice. For large organisations, it means letting go of language or processes that are well understood by everyone – except the people who actually matter. Your users.

Design often gets called UX in a digital world. UX stands for user experience. But, like communications, in a truly user-centred organisation everyone is responsible for the user experience. If the service is terrible because the server speed is slow, because of a legacy contract signed 10 years ago – no amount of design or UX can fix that. Designing the best possible user experience is therefore the responsibility of everyone on the team.

The design of public services often ends up taking a form that makes little sense to anyone but public servants and their peers. The ability of technocrats to craft services in a way that meets the needs of their entire customer base or citizenry is a far more compromised affair. Most government or corporate websites look awful because someone has planned for two weeks of UX at the end of a two-year project. That's putting lipstick on a pig. It may meet the requirement of 'doing some design' but it won't made the user experience any better.

There are two perceptions of design that Ben and the GDS design team spent much of their first couple of years trying to eradicate from the organisation. Firstly, design is not marketing or communications. The primary role of design in your organisation is to make it easier for users to interact with, in the services it provides and information it publishes. Marketing is about persuading users that something is a good idea. Design is about making it self-evident.

Usability is better than persuasion, and often cheaper to boot.

Secondly, your organisation will probably need to tackle an unspoken class system in design. There's no rule that says that a government website has to look worse than a website for Apple, just because it's 'good enough for government'. Some of the best and most loved designs in history come from public sector projects: the 1970s' NASA identity guidelines were released as a hugely popular Kickstarter project. A digital organisation working in any sector should have high design ambitions.

As well as using design differently, you'll need a different type of designer. Good designers work side by side with user researchers and with developers. Good designers can code. Good designers are involved at every stage of a service, not just coming in at the beginning or the end.

You don't need creative directors and you don't need some dabbler from the finance department who's 'really into all that art and design stuff'. You need integration designers, front-end developers, graphic designers and service designers. Which designers the team needs depends on the service your organisation is building and where you are in the process.

Interaction designers work on the interactions throughout a service. Should this form be one page or split one question per page? What's easier for the user? They make prototypes.

Front-end developers code the front-end of a website, seen by the users. The best ones overlaps with back-end developers and the designers. They have a good eye for what works best for users.

Graphic designers think about the aspects of design that are perhaps more familiar; what font a website should use, or how to structure a page so it's easy to read. They can provide a vital link between interaction design and service design.

Service designers think about the whole service end to end. They can join all the parts together and often cross over with business analysts. They do this all with the user in mind.

As in modernist architecture, ornament is a crime in digital service design. When the UK's Department for Work and Pensions launched the Carers Allowance benefit service the analytics showed many people completing the form at 4 a.m. We asked users why this was, and the answer was that for many full-time carers it was the only time they got to themselves. In a context like this, there is no place for ornament.

That said, design need not become entirely functional. A digital organisation needs designers who understand the heritage of design in your country or company, and have a strong sense of the mission this work needs. Their ambition should be the same as when Henry Beck designed the Underground map. Their goal should be to place this project in the same canon as those great designs; not by pastiche or homage, but by using the principles of good design adopted by the organisation's pioneers.

If they do this well enough, digital teams can unlock design patterns their organisation has never faced before. In the UK's Ministry of Justice, a team redesigned the lasting power of attorney service following GDS's design principles. Soon after a beta version was launched, the department's call centre began getting more contacts. This was a puzzle and potentially a worry – the new service was supposed to reduce the number of people ringing up, not increase it. It turned out the spike in calls had been caused by users who wanted to praise the team on how smooth they found their experience. A positive feedback button was duly added to the online service.

What if a user doesn't know what they need?

The idea of designing for user needs can be a problem if the user doesn't appear to know what they need. In government, this paternalistic view is surprisingly common. It is also a bit of an excuse. Users may not always know (or care) that they need to pay certain taxes in exchange for certain services, but are well aware they need a public service that is simple and clear enough for them to complete it accurately and quickly so they can get on with their day. The user need of government services often boils down to 'I don't want to get into trouble.' Public services should provide that reassurance with the minimum of friction. They often fail in this.

In the corporate world, a well-worn route to success is to create demand for something that a user never knew they needed – but they are now desperate to pay for. The old Henry Ford quote that 'people would have asked for faster horses' is relevant here. How do you design in a user-centred way while overcoming that barrier?

The answer is essentially the same as for government. Your corporate strategy and the available technologies might seem like enough to determine what products or services you should go with, but you are flying blind without some sense of user need. Users might not know the shape of the product or service that they need, but they intuitively know they need it to have certain qualities. That might be speed of transaction, convenience or a set of functions. Finding how how much your users value these things, relatively speaking, will give you clues about how to build your offering.

Beauty at scale

Being disciplined about design has organisational benefits (saving the money and time that goes into creating different logos or websites for every individual department or business) and user benefits (a consistent look and feel are familiar, reassuring and easier to learn how to use). If a user only has to learn how one government online service works to understand how all government services will behave, that removes a lot of friction from the process.

For a digital team to create designs that work at scale, it must make it easier to work in their way than to build something different. There are two ways of doing this. You can impose a cost on teams elsewhere in the organisation choosing to design things differently by imposing rules and constraints on alternatives. Depending on your organisation's culture, you may need to use this stick. Ideally, though, you will offer a carrot.

Design patterns – small chunks of html that give templates for buttons or boxes, colour palettes, style guidelines, microcopy text – are ideal for this purpose. Creating and publishing these patterns create little pieces of utility that have been built and tested thoroughly, so others don't have to do the same. This makes the act of designing consistently good-looking services the path of least resistance, rather than additional effort. Start and end pages, drop-down boxes, layout, typography, colour and forms – all can be done once and shared.

Having created design patterns, the role of the digital team and design community across the organisation is to curate and improve them. Templates should not be considered to have been set in stone, so it must be straightforward for teams working on services across the organisation to easily get hold of (and apply) any improvements. Publishing your patterns in the open and creating a thriving community of designers to keep them fresh is the best way to make this happen.

SUMMARY

- Communications is part of delivery, not a separate discipline.
- Repeat a handful of crisp, short messages until they are widely understood.
- Create a simple and distinct communications style, and apply it to everything the team does.
- Build constructive relationships with journalists based on trust and reciprocity.
- Use the power of design to fundamentally change how your organisation does things, rather than making broken things look prettier.
- Good design requires good, dedicated designers, not enthusiastic hobbyists.

Chapter 11

Setting the standard

Digital teams trying to change their organisations are often labelled rule breakers. This is not true. Successful digital organisations don't abandon rules. They invent them.

Standards and manuals that codify digital ways of working have become a common feature of digital transformation. The UK government's digital service standard and manual – itself inspired by similar efforts in New Zealand – has been adapted around the world. Australia, Ontario and Scotland have created their own versions. The US Digital Service and 18F built a playbook. Digital agitators in local UK government are taking a similar approach.

Bureaucracies and big companies have rules for a reason. They are a cheap way of scaling behaviour, fast. No large organisation can run itself without some standardised processes. For slow-moving organisations carrying a lot of history on their minds, those rules will tend to solidify a particular way of working, for better or worse. In earlier chapters, we have talked about the need for digital teams to get a mandate that allows them to challenge these prevailing rules. This becomes necessary when organisations are stuck in ruts that run counter to the agility, openness and wariness of false certainty that a digital institution needs to adopt.

The chances are that lots of people within your organisation, from top to bottom, will be fed up with the rules and standards currently in place. Most people in big organisations intuitively feel that following bad rules is probably better than having no rules, and they are right. Mediocrity is better than chaos. But if people like to follow rules, write some new ones.

When it comes to rules, the role of a digital institution is to do two things. First, give the rest of the organisation the confidence to abandon the existing rules that are actively unhelpful or widely ignored. Second, and more importantly, to provide replacement standards that give the rest of the organisation clear cues about what good should look like. Doing the first without the second leads to chaos. Doing the second without the first leaves you with multiple sets of rules layered on top of each other, creating confusion and slowing everyone down.

Digital service standards

A service standard is a list of things that a team designing and running a digital service needs to be and needs to do. The how and the what are equally important. A service standard will value equally what skills are part of the team, the technology and design choices they make, and how they plan to measure service performance, along with other things.

The GDS launched its own digital-by-default service standard and accompanying service manual – which explained the expectations behind the standard in more detail – in 2013, about two years into the team's journey. The objective of the standard was ultimately to make all government digital services so good that people would prefer to carry out the task online. Every new service launching on GOV.UK had to pass the standard.

The service standard formalised how the GDS would apply one of its two levers of influence: domain power. As a team, the GDS had the final say about what was good enough to go on GOV.UK. As GOV.UK was the single domain for government, if you couldn't get on GOV.UK, you effectively couldn't run an online government service. Provided your digital team is in charge of a single domain, this domain power is a valuable lever for changing an organisation's behaviour. However, a service standard does not have to be based around domain power. It could easily be used as a gatekeeper for determining which teams are entitled to draw down on a specific source of internal funding, for example. If they want access to the money, a team needs to prove itself ready to make the best use of it.

In theory, the GDS didn't have to produce a service standard, or any new sets of rules. Nobody asked them to. The team could have simply told departments that their service was or wasn't permitted to launch on GOV.UK, without explaining the decision. With power comes responsibility. The chances of the GDS's government colleagues tolerating any capricious, inconsistent decision-making from the centre about what was acceptable were not good. It wouldn't have taken much bad behaviour for those powers to be taken away. Codifying a service standard was as much to protect the GDS from itself as it was to help the rest of organisation.

When the GDS started working on the standard, we thought the hard bit would be working out what should be included in it, and where the new rules should apply. That's easier than you'd think. The first version of the UK's digital service standard was written in half an hour, in a few spare minutes found in the midst of shepherding GOV.UK towards going live.

As the GDS began defining standards in more detail, we had to think more carefully about the outcome we wanted to achieve, and what defaults the standard needed to challenge. It is clearly important that your organisation's digital services can be regularly iterated and improved upon, based on user feedback. However, writing that down as a standard is only worth doing if you simultaneously ensure the organisation's working practices aren't preventing people from working in that way. For example, demanding that teams work to an agile development cycle while the rest of the organisation still expects teams to follow traditional governance – quarterly meetings, lots of meeting papers, and so on – creates tensions and nugatory work. Service standards are as much about how an organisation works as they are about what it delivers.

Codifying the best 'what and how' is more straightforward than you might think. There are now plenty of published service standards that provide a strong starting point; the GDS team borrowed shamelessly from others when they wrote the UK version. However, it is through actually delivering redesigned services you will refine what practices need the protection of new rules. Equally importantly, there will be many teams working in your organisation who already know exactly what needs to be done to deliver excellent digital services, have tried doggedly to do so for a long time despite the obstacles. They will tell you if you make the effort to listen. What most of these teams lack is the support and senior backing to make change stick. The responsibility for the digital team with responsibility for writing new rules is to find the people who want to do the right thing, and use the mandate they have to remove everything that gets in their way.

The GDS's service standard was not the first time a UK public organisation had written down how the government should look and feel on the web. Before starting to define the new standard in detail, the GDS dug up hundreds of pages of web standards and technical specifications scattered all over the place. Some of these had been published, some were languishing on intranet pages and some were in drawers. Many were several years old. Some directly contradicted one another. Your organisation probably has some of these too. If it takes a real effort to find the existing rules, it is safe to assume that few people are paying attention to them. To test that hypothesis, the GDS decided to take down all of the existing web pages on standards, and wait to see what would happen. Nobody noticed.

Prior to the GDS service standard, most of the government's rules on how to deliver digital services had been optional – departments could choose whether or not to follow them. They were not really rules so much as guidelines. For organisations that are resistant to change or have individual units that prize their autonomy over learning from colleagues' experience, mere guidelines aren't hard enough.

One of themes we keep returning to in this book is that big organisations run on inertia, resisting change in their direction and speed. If you're trying to set standards for what good looks like, to have a real impact, you have to deliver something that disrupts that inertia. To have real bite, rules need to be attached to powers. Powers enable a digital team to make choices and decisions. Decision makers are unpopular, because somebody tends to lose out. Look forward to becoming unpopular.

Unpopularity comes with the territory of a digital team in the process of writing new rules. This is uncomfortable, but consider the alternatives. Most bureaucracies are full of smart, reasonable and agreeable people. Their organisations provide very few personal incentives for them to challenge the equilibrium of culture, rules and manners currently in place. This often makes bureaucrats more quickly offended by breaches of etiquette than breaches of what is fair for citizens, voters or taxpayers. The latter still matters to them, but is made to feel abstract and distant by the hugeness of the organisation they work in. Good people end up on the side of the inertia, because their employer tacitly encourages them to keep the peace rather than making a colleague's life more difficult in the interest of users. Going against organisational etiquette doesn't mean throwing personal etiquette out the window; working for a disruptive digital team does not entitle you to be any less empathetic, open and aware of your colleagues. Nonetheless, successfully resisting organisational etiquette in favour of arguing on the user's behalf can lead to a digital team being perceived as the awkward squad.

The first goal for any new set of rules must be to prevent terrible things from happening. That means stopping projects that may have lots of momentum, money and egos attached. Everyone knows what these projects are like: juggernauts careering towards the cliff edge, or zombies that just won't die. Everyone knows they will fail. Everyone feels powerless to stop them. Faced with impending failure, writing down a list of guidelines you would like to see and keeping your fingers crossed they will be noticed is largely a waste of time. Dusty piles of optional guidelines and best practice manuals coexisting with numerous disasters are testament to this.

If your digital institution doesn't have hard powers – like the ability to stop spending, or prevent something being launched, or hand out crucial funding – it might be wisest to forget about setting new rules for the time being. Politically savvy executives and officials will quickly sniff out whether they have to listen to you in order to achieve their objectives. If they can route around you, the digital team should spend its time continuing to concentrate on delivering things that work first, and make them flock in your direction. Earn the right to be trusted as a good judge. If the digital team plays it right, someone will appoint them for the job before long.

RETROSPECTIVE: BENEFITS SYSTEM ONLINE

BESOL (Benefits System Online) was a digital service designed to show users the full set of benefit payments they received on a single online dashboard. It was led by the UK's Department for Work and Pensions (DWP), and delivered by a systems integrator.

By the time it reached the GDS, BESOL had already resisted multiple attempts at cancellation. A product of the previous administration, it had few political friends, yet still kept going. Previous reviews and assurance exercises failed to halt its momentum. The service had been in development for more than four years, running up a bill of well over £20 million. In that time, no part of it had been publicly tested.

The benefits policy landscape had meanwhile changed dramatically during the time the service was worked on. Much of the information BESOL was supposed to show users was no longer relevant, as many of the benefits were being replaced by a new Universal Credit (UC). UC was not planning to integrate with BESOL. Furthermore, many of the very old systems that BESOL plugged into to provide data did not operate at weekends. Users looking for information through BESOL on a Saturday or Sunday were guaranteed an inaccurate picture; a recipe for lots of irate and confused calls to DWP's contact centres. Having been picked up by the GDS's spending control process when making a relatively small bid (<£2m), the GDS had the opportunity to triage BESOL into an assessment against the digital service standard assessment. The service failed on the majority of the 26 points, and it quickly became clear that the supplier responsible for BESOL had no way to address most of them. While BESOL was fatally flawed, it had built up sufficient momentum and sunk cost in DWP to make it very hard for officials to stop. Spending controls allowed the digital team to step in and take joint responsibility for cancellation. It was difficult for DWP to do this alone, partly because there was not wide enough recognition of BESOL's failings within the department and partly because DWP's senior officials lacked the political cover to do so.

For now, let's say the digital team earns a mandate to set standards and assess teams from the organisation against them. Once these powers are established, it still takes some confidence to stand up and say 'we're not doing it that way anymore.' To land that kind of difficult conversation successfully, you'll need to bring others in the organisation with you. Having strong supporters for working in a new way who are ready to stand up when the arguments begin is essential, because those who have done well out of the previous arrangements will begin to realise the game has not changed in their favour.

For your supporters to trust you, they will need to be assured you can be trusted in your judgments of what makes for a good digital service, and that you appreciate the context they are working in. When making assessments of what is good and bad, be transparent about your reasoning. Be humble about mistaken judgment calls you make, and don't apologise for the fact you're learning as you go.

The digital team must avoid falling into the trap of rule-setters everywhere, which is to impose a way of doing things without providing any practical help for how to go about it. You should accompany the stick of digital standards with the best carrot you can provide, and make it easier to follow the rules than to ignore them. In the UK, the service standard would have not have succeeded without the design manual that accompanied it. The manual included design patterns, written guidance, job descriptions, links to communities of practice, and much more besides. It built goodwill, clarified meaning and created some collective ownership for what good looked like from right across the organisation.

It should not be for a few people in a central team to keep defining the new rules on their own – the wisdom of crowds will ultimately provide a far richer view. The role of the central digital institution as a setter of standards should evolve over time to becoming a chairperson: making sure discussions on what good looks like don't rumble on indefinitely without coming to a decision, and curating things that capture the current version of best practice. Keeping those discussions going requires effort – but it's one paid for by maintaining an up-to-date view of best practice, avoiding service failures and attracting good people to come and work with you. In the UK, the GDS service manual was left static for too long after it was launched. We didn't make enough of the opportunity it offered for celebrating the work going on out in departments. Those who have created service manuals and standards in the GDS mould should look after them.

Spending controls

The service standard was our way of codifying domain control, the first of the GDS's powers. The second power needed a different set of rules, designed to achieve a slightly different objective.

As well as managing GOV.UK, the GDS was also responsible for overseeing the UK government's spending on digital and technology projects, and giving approval for all spending above a certain amount. For digital projects, this started at zero – every change needed sign-off. Spending controls were brought in by the Cabinet Office minister, Francis Maude, initially as a means of curtailing the government's enormous IT bill. The government hypothesised – correctly, as it turns out – that the flow of cash could be reduced substantially while achieving better outcomes. The controls weren't exclusively about technology; the Cabinet Office under Francis Maude had a much wider efficiency and reform agenda, targeting fraud and error reduction, improving commercial outcomes, and sorting out the government's sprawling estate. Spending controls provided a pivot to lever change.

The digital service standard was fundamentally a creative control, designed to make it easier for teams all over government to build user-centred digital services to go on GOV.UK. Money was saved as a result of people moving from offline channels to the online version, as a result of the redesigned online service being preferable to use. The true measure of success was putting better services in front of millions of people.

The spending controls for digital and technology, on the other hand, were a destructive control. Success in terms of spending controls was measured in terms of money not spent as a result of consolidating, renegotiating or stopping supplier contracts that delivered poor value for the taxpayer. The UK had plenty of these to work on. It still does. In 2015, the UK advertised 167 public contracts of over €100m.

France, the EU nation with the next highest number, advertised just 29.[53]

Spending control rules were of a different nature to those in the service standard. Whereas the service standard was deliberately ambiguous in places to allow for best practice in digital service design changing over time, the spending control rules were much more definitive 'red lines'. They emphasised avoiding practices that were widely recognised as being a bad idea, yet still kept happening in the organisation. The service standard was operating nearer the edges of what was new, and therefore allowed for the fact the GDS couldn't have all the answers. The spend controls codified relatively well-known principles that had simply been overlooked by the organisation for years.

To take one example – the technology spend controls forbade any government contracts for IT exceeding a total lifetime value of £100 million. £100 million is a lot of IT. For several years, the default behaviour in Whitehall was to let out very expensive multi-year contracts to large technology consultancies. These arrangements turned up repeatedly at the scene of major public sector disaster stories. The technology spending controls, with ministerial backing, put a block on them.

Spending controls often cannot afford to adopt the relative fluidity of the service standard. An organisation's IT spending can become so out of hand that the remedial work needs to be equally extreme. The other reason for being definitive was that the nature of technology contracting in government was such that one had to be ready to make big improvements at the first opportunity you got. Many IT contracts in government ran for for 5, 7 or even 10 years. Miss the chance to get better value for money in the current negotiation, and you may not get the chance again until the next parliamentary term, or the one after that.

Any large organisation with growing IT costs needs to recognise that it is running against market trends; the cost of established technology is falling, and the last thing an organisation needs is to buy even more of it. If you want the same outcomes for your business, your IT should get cheaper. If you want outcomes that improve at the same rate as technology evolves, the cost should stay broadly the same. And if you want to be at the bleeding edge, you should make very sure you are making a wise investment.

Running assessments

The biggest test for a digital standard or spending control is the first project that it stops. Sooner or later, you'll be confronted with a juggernaut, the IT programme that has already spent millions and is widely known to be a disaster-in-waiting. Your new standard will be in the spotlight as the only thing that could realistically stop it, or at least force the programme on to a better path. When that moment comes, follow your process properly. Don't be tempted to duck the issue, and make special exemptions. Your new rules will be finished if you do.

If a service brought for assessment isn't good enough, the digital team must say so. Be human about it. These may be things that teams have worked on for years. Don't be high-handed. Don't crow. Don't patronise. Make the most of the senior support you have prepared in advance. It will be painful, it will take a long time – but the first project a digital team stops represents a line in the sand. You are saying politely: this is no longer acceptable. Remember that if you capitulate at this early stage, inertia will barrel on.

For both spending controls and the service standard, the rules themselves are only half of the story. To really change the weather, you need to change the people.

As we said in chapter 7, for many large organisations, decisions about technology have been sidelined to the point that IT almost behaves like a separate entity to the rest of the business. When it comes to making a strategic appraisal of an investment in technology, or the effectiveness of a new online service, there are very few people in the business who possess the knowledge or interest to give an informed view. At its worst, this leads businesses and government departments to make costly decisions about technology entirely independently of the strategic or policy goals they are trying to achieve. Executives are then perplexed as to why their expensive new systems don't work. Sidelining IT makes it easier to blame them, rather than the leadership, when everything goes wrong. In reality, technology failure is organisational failure.

The most radical impact of spending controls and the service standard comes not from the rules themselves, but from the people they empowered to make strategic decisions about the business of government. Those responsible for making decisions over the wisdom of a technology investment or digital service should be people who deeply understand technology or have built digital services. This sounds obvious, but is often not the case. Rather than clever generalists looking at forms, appraisals and assessments were led by multidisciplinary panels of specialist experts unafraid of putting a few noses out of joint, not generalists with one eye on their career.

When setting up the governance and process around rules and controls, there is often a case made for assigning a full-time team to run assessments. This instinct is reasonable; to successfully run this kind of process across a huge organisation you need a small central team – a handful of people – to manage the logistics, maintain consistency and ensure the rules and standards are kept up-to-date. The job of assessing, however, should be spread across the widest range of qualified people in your organisation as possible. When assessing a digital service against your standard, the people on both sides of the table should be those who have some experience of delivering those services. For the digital specialists in your organisation, taking part in assessing the work of others should be part of the day job, but not their whole job.

The problem with having anyone spending their whole time as an inspector or assessor is that they risk blunting their experience of delivery realities – the very thing that makes them an effective, empathetic judge of a service's quality in the first place. Equally, asking someone with no experience or awareness of the technology market to make a judgement on how sensible it is to put out a tender for a five-year contract on cloud hosting or data centres is not a good idea.

Creating new rules and standards allows you to scale practices across an organisation quickly. Putting the assessment of teams in the hands of qualified, multidisciplinary groups of specialists allows you to ensure those practices remain sound.

The butterfly effect

The biggest risk that comes with setting new rules is that they come to resemble what they were designed to replace. Setting new rules doesn't stop inertia from being the defining characteristic of your big organisation; it merely nudges the direction of travel. Unless you keep them fit for purpose, your new rules can quickly turn into next year's cumbersome processes.

The problem that all bureaucracies face is that it becomes very hard for any process to become smaller or shorter. Without constant vigilance, they just accrete and grow. Every extra page added to a rule book may be a completely sensible step, in and of itself. Each time a new and unanticipated problem occurs, the natural response is to add another rule or standard to stop it from happening again. Big organisations like rules, remember. However, if they follow that instinct every time, an ungainly monster will emerge.

The GDS encountered the issue of rule-creep within a couple of years of the digital service standard being set up. The first assessment of a team and their work against the standard took 25 minutes, covered three points, involved four people and resulted in one email. Two years later, a typical assessment against the standard took four hours, covered 18 points, involved 10 people and resulted in a chunky report and lengthy email exchange. That doesn't mean the latter is a broken version of the process. The later assessments against the standard yielded far richer feedback, more informed teams, and better services for users. However, that thoroughness comes at the cost of speed.

There is no perfect answer to getting the right balance of speed and thoroughness. Sometimes a digital team should operate in a way that is consciously challenging and disrupting the prevailing culture of its organisation, after achieving a big, public success, say, or in its early days. As a general rule, the culture of most large organisations values thoroughness over speed. When the digital team's star is riding high, standards and controls should operate in the most rapid and light-touch a way as possible – whatever is most countercultural. In other, riskier periods, where the digital team should be more circumspect, applying more thoroughness to the assessment process is a wise move. The approach to applying standards should be flexed according to context. It is worth remembering that it is always easier to sell greater thoroughness over greater speed in big organisations. A digital team should be careful not to give up its ability to move fast.

A second issue to consider is what a digital team excludes from standards in order to keep them as light as possible. Again, the wider organisation is likely to push in the direction of comprehensiveness without necessarily valuing the pace that this sacrifices. This is part of the reason that so many rules in a large organisation cut across each other; officials would rather risk confusing people by asking for three versions of the same form than risk not having one filled in at all.

When writing new organisational rules, don't include standards on topics that are already default behaviours. There's no point telling teams to do certain things they're already inclined towards doing, because other incentives in the organisation are already pulling them that way. Writing business cases is a good example of something that didn't need to be in a digital service standard; the bias towards such analysis is strong enough already.

SUMMARY

- New rules can change organisational behaviour on a large scale, quickly.
- Spending controls run by technologically literate assessors are the single most effective tool for saving money through digital transformation.

- Give standards and controls the power to stop bad projects, and use it consistently.
- Processes expand over time; make digital standards as light-touch as possible.
- Those assessing teams against standards and spending controls must understand delivery, rather than being full-time standard setters.

Chapter 12

Finding leaders

Just as it would not be acceptable for a Minister not to
understand how her departmental budget works, it is not
acceptable for her not to understand how technology affects
her brief.

— Martha Lane Fox

The model of digital transformation we have described in
this book is one driven from the heart of an organisation;
a powerful centre providing momentum to change the whole.
The journeys taken by specialists from periphery to acceptance in large organisations is similar; be they statisticians,
scientists or economists, all needed a strong, coherent voice
in the bureaucracy's centre before they gained widespread
acceptance. Unfocused collaboration did not provide that.
Digital is no different.

However, gripping change from the centre is a strategy
that can only been sustained for so long. The influence of a
powerful central unit in most big organisations fluctuates
over time, oscillating from all-powerful to virtual bystander.
Controlling everything from the centre is not sustainable nor
desirable forever, though this will come as news to a handful
of all-powerful ministries like the UK's Treasury. To embed the
new course set by a central digital team before you run out of
political capital or burn out with exhaustion, you will need to

bring in leaders who can take forward the agenda elsewhere. They are the ones who will ensure the departments or business units can stay the course.

A lack of technologically literate leadership has long been a structural weakness for public institutions as well as for many private corporations. At the executive level of the UK civil service, there has been very little expectation of basic technology knowledge from senior leaders. Officials could publicly confess to knowing nothing about technology without fear; professing a similar level of ignorance in finance or economics would simply not fly. Worryingly, many of these leaders have been equally candid about having little interest in remedying this weak spot. Not knowing is forgivable. Not having the curiosity to address the weakness is much less so.

This is not exclusively a government problem either, and many private enterprises are even more reluctant to acknowledge it. In our experience on both sides of the fence, the bar of technology embarrassment among leaders remains remarkably low in most large, legacy-driven organisations. Almost every major company of long standing will have a number of senior managers on the books that print off every email they are sent. Everyone still experiences meetings lengthened by 15 minutes while the attendees mess around with the overhead projector settings. This is normalised by leaders who accept technological incompetence as being OK. Imagine the same breezy amateurism applied to, say, accounting. You would expect a few costly, embarrassing mistakes as a result. It's a wonder there aren't more IT disasters.

The problems created by technology-incurious leaders are legion. They set a cultural expectation within the organisation that technology is no more than a question of plumbing – pipes and wires that can be ignored (unless something goes wrong) while the grown-ups deal with the real strategic issues. Ambitious juniors take note of this attitude, and grow to see technology projects as a path to a stalled career. Any capability or interest the organisation had in technology ebbs away.

This, in turn, leaves the organisation helpless in the face of technology suppliers, who need no excuse to gently ease large amounts of money in their direction. Don't blame the suppliers for their rapacity – they are merely following the incentives put in front of them – large bureaucracies are culpable for creating a scenario where they have outsourced their ability to make sensible decisions about technology.

When it comes to technology leadership, one task for the digital team tends to be a tough one – getting rid of the actively useless. If the generation of chief information officers (CIOs) or IT directors in your organisation is the biggest blocker to digital transformation, prepare for some hard conversations.

The goal is not to move on people who disagree with you. Dissenting voices based on experience and knowledge of the legacy you're stepping into are valuable, and should be kept at all costs. Constructive scepticism will allow the digital team to identify and address traps they may otherwise miss. The layer you need to remove is those leaders whose view is devoid of curiosity and openness. These are the people who will make every miniscule step forward a battle. Left unchecked they will tire you out, and see you off. There's no way to teach, coach or circumvent your way around them. Find them an exit.

The first wave

Before getting into the more painful conversations required to shake up the organisation's technology leadership from within, the digital institution first needs to establish a group of departmental leaders.

Putting some structure around the relationship between the central team and the departments is an important early task. There are very practical reasons for this. Creating a group of people who are empowered to represent all the various parts of the organisation keeps the number of conversations the digital team has to handle with the rest of the business to a manageable number.

Good candidates for this first group of digital leaders are people one step away from board level in their department: senior enough to carry their organisation's view, but not so far up in the boardroom echelons that they're unlikely to turn up to any of the meetings. In the first year of transformation, a department's digital leader tends to be a self-selecting position; if they're curious and optimistic enough to take on the role, they're likely to be a decent candidate.

In the UK government, the group of departmental digital leaders met monthly. Unusually for a governance meeting in government, the first meeting opened up with an honest admission – it wasn't certain what decisions the group would be making. What was certain was that it would be making some decisions that applied across the whole of central government; this was not a talking shop. It was not always for the centre to set the agenda or outcome of these meetings; departments that disagreed would work out their differences between themselves and report back, rather than have the central digital team pick a winner.

The value of setting up a Digital Leaders group was two-fold. Not only did it create a single decision-making body for digital issues that had representatives from right across the organisation, it also provided a licence for shutting down the plethora of digital and technology meetings that had proliferated. This is a good general rule for the first two years of a digital institution: never start a new regular meeting without shutting down at least two existing meetings.

Internet-era leaders

Having established effective governance, the next task is to bring in a new type of technology leader to operate at department or company board level. Some of these may already exist among your first group of digital leaders, and others will be elsewhere in your organisation. However, there is a good chance you will need to look outside for talent too. You will need two different types of leader.

Chief Digital Officer

The Chief Digital Officer (CDO) is the individual responsible for the user's end-to-end experience of the organisation. As far as the outside world is concerned, they are the person ultimately accountable for ensuring the services provided by the department are simpler, clearer and faster for users. They work first time. They are clear. Online transactions join seamlessly with any offline stages. An alternative is provided for those unable to use the web.

WIthin the organisation, the CDO is the loudest voice on the board speaking up on behalf of the user. They will also be the strongest advocate and backer for the digital ways of working we've outlined in earlier chapters: agile, multidisciplinary, bringing together digital skills with more traditional corporate competencies. They will support and educate the board on the practices and operating models of the internet era that they may not be familiar with.

Being a Chief Digital Officer is a big job. It can also be a tricky one to land within a traditional executive committee. In a government department, the board may include separate directors of policy and operations (two disciplines that digital explicitly brings together), or directors of specific policy areas (which digital services may cut across). A CDO is a horizontal role, working across an organisation much like a Chief Finance Officer would. However, it is also integral to what the vertical business or policy lines are doing. A CDO presents fundamental challenges to the legacy structure of a big organisation. This is not an accident. However, that does make it a difficult and sometimes isolating position, and not an easy one to stick.

Nonetheless, being tenacious in forcing this structural conversation at the top of an organisation is one of the key roles for a CDO. There are two ways of ducking it, and neither turn out well. In the first case, the CDO ends up running a business or policy area – effectively looking after one of the verticals. This allows them to transform one bit of the organisation, but leaves the rest of it largely untouched. The other option – operating as a central function along the top of an organisation, like a finance or HR department – runs the risk of becoming peripheral and getting stuck in the world of 'innovation'. Chief Innovation Officers produce delightful prototypes and alphas. They generate excitement and demonstrate the possibilities of change to an organisation. But can they actually change the business? Be wary of becoming a Chief Innovation Officer.

Chief Technology Officer

If the role of the CDO is to open the organisation's eyes to the why and how of transformation, the CTO is there to bring deep technology knowledge back into the heart of the strategic conversation.

When faced with technology questions with fundamental implications for their businesses – moving data into the public cloud, investing in new systems, experimenting with artificial intelligence or Merkel tree encryption – far too many executives are forced to basically guess. For advice they are left to rely on technology suppliers (who are not the most neutral observers), management consultants (ditto), tech-utopian or tech-phobic articles they've read, or the managerial instincts that have served them to date. None of these guides could be described as foolproof.

The CTO's role is not really to stop the board from making decisions that are idiotic; any candidate worthy of the CTO title will steer well clear of outright incompetence. No, the CTO is there to guide the board away from making decisive calls that are logical to people with a limited understanding of technology and the market conditions associated with it, but are clearly dangerous to somebody in the know. For example, buying a new proprietary HR and finance system on a five-year deal from a supplier that the department has already worked with for ten years might seem sensible to a non-technologist. The fact that the system is a complete pain to use (and ruinously expensive) may just about crop up on the leadership radar. What may not is the fact that systems like this are likely to become commoditised – which is to say, cheap and easily swapped with similar alternatives – in less than five years. Through a combination of ignorance and inertia, the department would be locking itself into the wrong deal, and constraining itself strategically as a result. A CTO stops this kind of mistake.

Externally, the CTO's role is more subtle than that of the CDO, who must take the rap for how the organisation presents itself online. The CTO's primary external function is to publicly demonstrate – through attending conferences and meetups, blogging and open communication – that their government department or organisation can be taken seriously by people who genuinely understand technology. As a recruitment message, that's a great deal more than most big companies can offer.

Finding new leaders

The old cliché says that the definition of madness is doing the same thing on different occasions and expecting different results. The way most organisations recruit digital and technology leaders is mad.

One of the most valuable things a central digital team can do is to help change this. As a large, legacy-laden organisation, you're unlikely to find your internet-era leaders by following typical search tactics. Nor will you persuade them to join you with the usual banquet of benefits. Bringing in these people will require more flexibility and a little creativity.

The first place to look is within your own organisation. This may be a non-starter if you have outsourced all your capability for technology and transformation. But on the latter, in particular, you might well be lucky. Don't just look for the known high-flyers. You should be looking for the angry people, those with ability and drive who have become intensely frustrated with the organisation's technological or cultural pathologies. They will know where the bodies are buried, and have already come up with the workarounds for failing corporate policies. Challenge them to create a working environment that doesn't drive them away, and promise them the space to have a proper go.

If not enough people can be found from within, you'll have to go searching for them. This is not an easy task. The number of people with the right set of skills to digitally transform large organisations is small, though growing. The temptation is to try poaching somebody from one of the Silicon Valley digital giants. Depending on the individual, that might be the right call. However, don't be taken in by the brand. Amazon, Facebook and the like are mighty companies, but they were digital from the beginning. You are not. The challenge of moving a legacy organisation to the internet era offers a different set of problems.

Look for companies and institutions who have changed their character and business within a context that works for them. Delve into your networks. As board-level players, having a bond of trust with your new CDO and CTO is essential if they are to bring to the table what you need. Having them as a known quantity, second- or third-hand, can be a helpful start.

For their part, prospective CDOs and CTOs joining from outside your organisation will be testing the water with you for signs of the conditions we covered in the earlier chapters of this book. By joining your organisation, they are taking a gamble with their careers. They will want to know more about what has precipitated the job being advertised in the first place. Where's the crisis? What are they, personally, expected to do about it?

They will be looking for strong leadership, at political or top-tier executive level. Meetings with the minister or CEO to give a candidate the chance to look into the whites of their new boss's eyes will count for a lot more than chats with a HR director who doesn't quite follow why they are hiring a CDO anyway.

One of the biggest worries for organisations who recognise the need to hire internet-era leadership is that they won't be able to afford them. We have seen governments baulk at the very idea of bringing in CDOs and CTOs because of the perceived cost. These skills are scarce, and in demand. They will not be cheap. However, the truth lying behind this fear is not really about pay.

Public institutions in particular have a fantastic card to play when it comes to attracting leaders: their mission. Several brilliant people who saw the GDS's open communications contacted the team directly to ask if they could join in. It's hard to offer bigger, more impactful problems to work on than what a government department will typically tackle on a daily basis. However, the executive benefits package of most public sector organisations – relatively low pay, relatively high job security, pensions and holidays – all appeals to a certain type of person at a particular stage of their careers. The profile of many prospective CDOs and CTOs doesn't fit this. They may prefer to do shorter, high-intensity stints of three to five years in a job before moving on. The career incentives for officials discourage this. To bring in internet-era leaders to government – and indeed, most traditional hierarchy-led organisations – means unpicking the benefits package.

Many governments know this. But perversely, rather than looking at the structural issue putting off this kind of talent from joining their organisation, they have instead defaulted to hiring interim consultants to do a more expensive job of the role a permanent CTO could fill. This exact problem is replicated all the way down through digital (and other) specialists at all levels of the organisation. These interim solutions are more expensive and leave little knowledge behind in the institution. Yet they persist because the pots of money assigned for consultants and permanent staff are separate. There is no logic to this.

Finding your new leaders is not easy, and only half the battle. Making your organisation ready to receive them in is equally important.

SUMMARY

- Too many senior leaders still don't care that they know very little about technology.
- Create a simple, decision-making governance that empowers departmental digital leaders and scraps dysfunctional meetings.
- Bring genuine technologists into executive-level positions to stop strategic errors.
- Don't parachute new executives or senior officials into departments and assume they will thrive; work to create the right conditions before they arrive.

Chapter 13

What comes next

If you've made it this far in building your digital institution, you've done well. A thriving digital institution at the centre of your organisation, energetic leaders in departments and new digital ways of working beginning to take hold at scale; all these things are substantial victories. Some of what you've done would have been considered impossible a couple of years ago. Taken together, this progress will change your organisation for the better. Users will notice the effects on the services you deliver. So will your colleagues. It is now more of an effort for your organisation to go back to the bad old ways than it is for it to stick to the course. Inertia is finally starting to tip in your favour.

The next stage comes down to tackling the most fundamental changes the Internet era will bring for post-industrial bureaucracies, and in particular, how accountability, money and risk will be managed. For public organisations, these questions shape the foundations of democratic institutions. Few companies – and no governments – have completed this final step. We are confident that the country that gets there first will win a big prize.

Because nobody has yet got to the finishing post, it is impossible to be certain exactly what the full set of practical steps to get there will be. In this final chapter, we have made a few suggestions for what an established digital team at this stage is likely to encounter in the future.

Doing less

Having shown that digital transformation of existing services is both possible and worth doing, the chances are that deep exhaustion will now be creeping into your team. Change is physically and mentally draining, the conflict it brings especially so. Digital transformation of any large organisation is tiring, partly because it is about loss. If you are to succeed in delivering the changes you want, various roles, processes and practices will end up being consigned to the past. For people coping with that loss, especially if it feels out of their control, there is a limit in how far they can stay with you.

Ignoring the health effects of organisational change is a mistake. Poor physical and mental health, exacerbated by professional stress, hurts people. It also kills organisations. There will be a moment in your transformation – certainly after no more than two years of long hours and hard work – where the digital team must take stock to address the debt it has accumulated from running fast. Some of that debt will be technical. Flaky code thrown together for the sake of delivery speed at the expense of scalability and elegance will need revisiting. So will sketchy design patterns, hacked processes and tatty office space. However, much of the debt will be human. The steady drip of stress takes a toll. Take time to recuperate, replenish, and go again. We regret not doing this more when we were working in government.

All of the digital team will need to replenish their energy for what is to come. By this stage, a good few people in your organisation may consider the team's work as largely done. As far as they're concerned, it has launched a few decent digital services, and saved a chunk of money. Mission accomplished. You've annoyed people on the way of course – that's a pity – so they think that perhaps now is the moment to consolidate the success and slow things down. If the digital team is all too tired to keep going, those keen to go back to an easy life will push back.

Resisting the hype

Every business strategy presentation for the last two years (and the next three) will have a slide that says something like: 'AI, blockchain, Internet of Things – what should we do?' For most organisations, this discussion is a little premature.

Even allowing for the fact these technology break-throughs are near the top of their hype cycle at the time of writing, we are not saying that they are unimportant for large organisations, public or private. Far from it. We're confident that artificial intelligence, connected devices and advances in cryptography will change the world, in predictable and unexpected ways. There are many excellent books, talks and blogs that do these subjects far better justice than we have the space to here.

However, for the purposes of digital transformation, we're unconvinced that organisations unable to provide their employees with a reliable system for filing their travel expenses should be betting the house on nailing the implications of artificial intelligence. Don't try to put the fire out with more petrol.

To a certain type of technocrat, innovations offer an irre-sistible opportunity to do a lot more talking at the expense of doing. It is noticeable that technologies like blockchain and artificial intelligence have especially gripped executives in organisations that have largely failed to react to the open internet's impact. In our experience, the more senior the figure, the more interested they are in technologies at the bleeding edge of discovery. On one level, this seems counterintuitive. Why would senior leaders with a track record of not applying more obvious and understood trends suddenly jump on the singularity bandwagon?

The answer, we suspect, is that technologies like blockchain and AI are for the most part still largely in the realm of theory. Delivery is not yet well-understood or demonstrable at scale. Very few companies (let alone established public institutions) have either the volume or sufficient structure to their data that would allow them to create a base of information that machine algorithms are able to 'learn' from. Their data is either unreliable, disparate or simply not there. Without fixing the foundations first, adding yet more new technologies to the mix in a legacy organisation is a recipe for adding yet more complexity.

Unaware or uninterested in this, some executives – especially those in policy-led government bureaucracies – feel comfortable with having an abstract debate about the consequences of, say, big data and connected devices. This intellectual workout takes place as they simultaneously fail to engage with the possibility of delivering real-life applications of well-understood technology.

A cynic might argue that these leaders have simply grown used to the idea that having a conversation is tantamount to doing something. That's probably unfair. The more likely culprit is a legacy bureaucratic culture that allows for excellent, rich, paper-based discussions among technophiles. Clever officials or strategists can draft many beautiful position papers about the prospects a new technology may hold for public life or future profitability. However, their organisation generally legislates against doing anything experimental with those technologies to test their assumptions against reality.

The answer to the technophile paradox is not to throw these new technologies off the agenda completely. AI is not going away. Ignoring it altogether is a more dangerous strategy than becoming distracted by its potential. However, in considering the disruptive possibilities of new technology, governments and corporate bodies would be wise to think about how well their organisation is arranged to make the most of them. If the culture, people and working practices of the institution are still grounded in principles that were set down in the age of the telegraph, the chances of responding with the requisite flexibility and agility to machine learning are slim. How can you be sure you're not buying snake oil? Which roles and professions should be part of the conversation? Which start looking obsolete? Can you buy into the business models that AI or data science services will use? If you've failed to get through the first digital transformation of your organisation, you will also fail to make the best of the second.

RETROSPECTIVE: PAPERLESS DRIVING

For all the cold water we are pouring on them in this chapter, AI and machine learning represent a new frontier. For government, they may even be more important to the development of public services than the internet itself. AI and machine learning can upend long-established government processes and systems and – more importantly – transform citizen outcomes by making public services ever more frictionless. For an organisation to make the best use of AI, it is very likely they will have already spent a lot of time and energy trying to take friction out of existing services. In the process of doing so, they will have fundamentally changed how their organisation works, preparing it to make better use of increasingly innovative technology.

DVLA, the UK's motoring agency, is a good example. In 2010, DVLA was a laggard for IT in government. It was ruinously expensive and dangerously complacent. So ingrained were the incumbent IT suppliers, they literally had a seat on the board. DVLA's head office in Swansea had space to accommodate 10 enormous articulated lorries, each one bringing tonnes of paper through the doors every day.

Thanks to the tireless work of many people, the DVLA took the difficult steps needed to bring technology skills in-house. In the process, it was bold enough to scrap both the paper car tax disc and the paper counterpart driving licence, with relatively few hiccups along the way.

On the surface of it, simply getting rid of ancient forms would appear to have little to do with the possibilities in applying AI and machine-learning principles to driving. This technology would, for example, give a minister the ability to incorporate real-time data of every driver in the country into a digital driving licence. In a situation where elderly drivers were causing fatal accidents, the minister could advocate for digital driving licences based on an individual's personal driving style or health – alcohol levels, blood pressure – accessed via the driver's phone or smart watch. The AI would then decide if that individual was safe to drive that day. The direction a government chooses to take with AI is as much a political choice as it is a technological one, but it is so far removed from the old paperwork as to feel like an entirely separate conversation.

These two perspectives are united by one thing – the institution responsible for making them happen. DVLA's digital efforts to date have exemplified two things: getting the organisation to focus on making services frictionless for the user's benefit, and putting in place the multidisciplinary teams that could deliver them. This combination of attitude and capability is what made true innovation possible, and opened the door to delivering fully digital licences in the future. Without the recognising the crisis the organisation faced, the DVLA would not have got close to this position. The chances of it delivering artful machine-learning-led services without fundamentally changing the institution itself are slim to none too.

One indicator of an organisation's maturity and readiness for this next wave of technologies – assuming that it already has a digital working culture in place – is how it looks after its data. If an institution knows what data it owns, makes it machine readable, and has considered the data protection and privacy issues that come with the responsibility of looking after it, it might have a fighting chance. Without those things, forget it.

Whatever the hype may be, new technologies like machine learning are forcing the right questions into the open. Lying beneath most of them is the fundamental issue of trust. To move from transforming services to transforming the organisation, you need to look with a fresh eye at the balance of trust, accountability and power.

Government as a platform

In the UK government – and many others – the path of bureaucratic power is a vertical one. The British constitution is a famously flexible thing (proving that the Establishment has no problem with an iterative, agile approach when you really come down to it), but certain conventions are fixed. Put very simply, prime ministers are accountable to parliament for the collective performance of their ministers. Ministers are accountable to parliament for the collective performance of their departments. Parliament is accountable to the voters.

Straightforward enough. The bureaucracy, too, is accountable to parliament, with various committees assigned to holding each department to account.

The unit of government organisation in this system is the department. It is the department that is given money, determines how it runs itself, and owns the policy. It is the minister of that department who makes decisions. The slight kink in this model is the senior civil service – the 3,000 or so top officials – who are technically managed by a central department, the Cabinet Office. Nonetheless, the large majority are assigned to departments, and behave as if owned by them.

All this context is needed to explain that government works best when it is trying to deliver something through one department. When that happens, the money, control, responsibility and accountability all align in a single management chain. This doesn't guarantee success. The organisational, management or political pathologies of individual departments can easily scupper things. As a rule, though, the more departments get involved, the more difficult it becomes to get things done.

The departmental model is not necessarily broken. Look at pretty much any advanced economy around the world, and the government departments almost invariably have the same names: health, education, interior ministry, and so on. This equilibrium also suggests that the buckets of policy activity that governments split themselves into are, if not right, probably a fair attempt at being the least wrong.

Where the departmental model demonstrably fails is in delivering things that all departments need. All the incentives guide departments towards thinking they are special when it comes to, say, building a system that can handle appointment booking, or buying laptop computers for staff. Even if they recognise they aren't that special, there is no reason for a senior leader of the Department of Pencils to say, 'We'll rely on the Department of Pens to sort this out for us.' If Pens does a bad enough job to cause Pencils' service to fail, who takes the rap? Pencils.

The departmental arrangement of accountability – and the lack of trust that quietly festers between those separate institutions – is most obvious in government, but applies equally in many large, federated companies. This is especially obvious in conglomerates, where different CEOs consider their company to be their domain, and see sharing with others in the group as risky business.

Bringing us back to digital transformation, it is easy to see the problem. Transforming services and applying digital ways of working to individual departments is not an easy task, but a relatively manageable one, given the clearer chain of accountability. Transforming the entire organisation into a genuinely user-centred one is a whole different puzzle. Users don't particularly care which department provides them their service. They just want it to work. Taxpayers and shareholders don't care who builds or buys the system that handles online payments. They just don't want to see the organisation paying separately for 30 versions of the same thing.

Most of the digital companies that have grown to dominate the global economy are platforms. They provide the infrastructure for whole markets to build themselves upon, and take a small cut off the millions that use them. This is true in taxis, holiday accommodation, advertising, news, retail, and many more besides. The biggest companies in all of these sectors often don't own stock or property. They own the market place.

For government, the opportunities in building platforms like these are real. Most public services are made of online and offline components that have been rebuilt or bought hundreds of times at the public's expense. Making payments, taking payments, publishing information, progress notifications through text and email, appointment booking, licences, grant applications. How great it would be if you could build these things once and have hundreds of public organisations using them, while steadily improving the service over time.

The UK tried, with qualified success, to bring platforms into government. Some of them, like GOV.UK, a central platform for publishing government information, worked very well. The UK is still working on platforms for payments, notifications and identity management, among others. At the time of writing, all of these have an uncertain future.

The threat to the status quo presented by platforms is that they erode the idea of departments as the organising framework of government, and replace it with something more attuned to what users of public services expect. Some view this as the thin end of a wedge that inevitably concludes with breaking constitutional norms. A legitimate charge laid by opponents of platform thinking is that it isn't entirely clear exactly what would replace the old structure. That is a little unfair; the full implications of departmentalism were far from understood when that route was chosen. The resistance the GDS encountered, however, tended to be less reflective. Known inefficiency was considered by many in the administrative side of government to be less scary than an unknown future. Senior bureaucrats are largely untouched by the consequences of their choices. That several of them would rather preserve conventions over the opportunity to deliver decent services they will never use is disappointing, but perhaps unsurprising. Those conventions got them where they are today.

So what gives platforms, and therefore the genuine transformation of a legacy-led organisation into one ready for the internet era, a chance of success? We can't say for certain, but there are at least five steps to getting closer.

Data registers

Common platforms are the public face of platform government: the component parts of services users see and use. The less glamorous side is the data architecture that sits under the services built from these components.

Creating accurate lists may sound like a prosaic task, but replacing the confused, duplicatory and inaccurate data architecture most old organisations sit on with new, canonical data sources is probably even more important than the user-facing platforms. Having single, accurate, trusted sources of information for all parts of the business or government to refer to cuts out many of the mistakes and burden of data re-entry for users.

For most bureaucracies, creating reliable data registers sounds like an unpleasant and near-endless job. It may take a decade to complete the transition from the patchwork of incompatible sources and false information to an architecture a digital native company would recognise as worth having. The longer it gets put off, the further you are from becoming a successful platform organisation.

The good news is that you can start small. Until very recently, the UK government didn't have a single agreed list of countries. Instead, there were scores of lists, some out of date, some incomplete, some with alternative names. The lack of consistency is maddening enough for people, but more crucially, makes the reliable use of machine-readable data near impossible. A register of single countries is now available for every department to use. It's a start.

Central power

The role of the centre in a platform government is up for debate. Most of the argument centres on what role a central department or institution should be responsible for designing and running platforms, versus playing a convener, standard-setting role, versus butting out and gently encouraging departments to play nicely. In the UK case at least, a century and a half of the last option has failed to deliver cross-organisation platforms that work.

Whether the centre plays a role in directly delivering platforms – whether that be building them itself or coordinating their purchase from suppliers – is harder to answer. Our instinct is that the central digital institution should take the lead in delivering at least some common platforms. The primary reason for this is that leaving the centre to chairmanship blunts its own delivery muscles. This makes it less sharp and credible in judging the quality of delivery elsewhere. Equally clearly, the centre can't do it all.

Accountability with control

Reach a certain level of seniority in government and you spend most of your life in meetings explaining or defending the work of others, many of whom you may have only met once or twice. The committee men and women (they are mostly men) are in a difficult position personally. While accountable, they have little or no control over what they carry the can for. This leads to the strange situation where the most qualified candidates for the top jobs are not those who deliver superlative projects, but those who can dance their way through trial by angry parliamentarians.

For platform government – or indeed, any form of digital government – to work, accountability and control need to be brought closer together. This may mean far more officials being called to explain their work in public and to parliament. It may also mean radically changing the way the legislature holds the bureaucracy to account. Perhaps moving away from the set-piece committee hearing – which lends itself to drama, defensiveness and post hoc rationalisation from MPs who rarely find themselves in possession of all the facts – would be a good idea. Having legislatures pivot towards a more regular conversation with public officials who are in charge of day-to-day delivery would make the accountability process a more valuable one.

Trust

Trust is the most precious commodity of the digital era. It is what makes the open internet work. Your organisation, be it government or corporate, will be forever hobbled if it is unable to trust itself.

When you strip away the pomp, process and procedure, an amazing number of the knots that bureaucracy ties itself in are largely down to the fact that senior officials trust neither their colleagues, nor their political bosses. A transparent government machine, built around platforms, would be a source of worry.

Until senior officials can trust each other enough to rely on one another's work, government as a platform cannot and will not happen.

A crisis of trust

For that change to happen, and the next phase of digital transformation to begin, we think another crisis will have to take place. Trust in democratic institutions is a fiendishly difficult thing to quantify. The real indicator that matters, though, is not trust as a blanket idea, but an organisation's trustworthiness to carry out a particular activity. You might trust your doctor, say, but you wouldn't necessarily trust him to fix your boiler.

There is a version of the future – a version where the transition to the digital era continues apace. People's expectations of what is possible continue to grow, yet deep political shocks leave surprisingly few marks on people's day-to-day experiences of the state. More people may step back and wonder: 'Should we trust this machine to deliver anything at all?'

Epilogue

This book has tried to explain that making large legacy organisations fit for the digital age is not complicated. Do not forget, however, that it is hard.

The biggest responsibility for any team trying to drive digital change is to keep learning. Iterate what you do, and how you do it. Recognise and correct your missteps, all the while focusing relentlessly on what your users need.

The GDS became an exemplar for governments and others trying to transform their analogue organisation into a digital one. That does not mean it was perfect. As an institution, the GDS itself can be described as a beta: a working prototype for how to transform a huge organisation, learning and improving as it went. It didn't get everything right the first time. What the UK team demonstrated should stop other governments and large organisations from making the same mistakes, but it may not.

Digital reformers will find their path inevitably brings them into conflict with other parts of the organisation. One person in the right place can do a great deal to unpick the hard work of hundreds. The differences come down to a very simple question. Are we going to organise ourselves around what our citizens, customers and users need? Or are we going to keep to the structures the organisation thinks it needs, based on fear, etiquette and inertia?

For as long as an organisation chooses to follow the latter path, it places a bet. An organisation serving its own needs is gambling that users will continue to accept what they are given, that they will acquiesce to a certain level of service, that people will continue to vote for the status quo – with their wallets or at the ballot box. It comes down to believing that while the internet may have changed the world, it needn't change their world.

Government bureaucracies and large organisations employ people who believe that they know better than the people they serve. Sometimes they do; that is why we put trust in institutions. When they don't know know better than the people they serve, and do not want to face the evidence that would force them to admit that, we all have a problem. Tackling over-confidence and denial is part of the job digital teams have to take on.

Becoming a digital organisation is a bet too. It is not free. It requires a significant investment of time, energy and people. It means diverting resources and downgrading other priorities. Often it means saying no. The difference for governments and organisations that invest in actively responding to an uncertain future is that the worst outcome is that they learn something. For those who stick incuriously to what they know, the worst outcome is they aren't needed anymore.

For companies, the rewards for being bold, curious and open to what comes next include survival, a competitive edge and access to the pick of the digital age's most precious commodity – talented, empathetic people.

For governments, the first nations to embrace the idea of a state organised on digital principles are likely to win the same profound rewards as those who had the foresight to reframe their institutions around the technological revolutions of the past. The rest of the world will then have to catch up.

Acknowledgements

A multidisciplinary team was needed to make this book happen.

Emer Coleman, Russell Davies and Giles Turnbull provided us with wise advice on the words, and made sure that we annoyed fewer people unnecessarily.

Diane Coyle was an excellent and patient editor (as well as being kind enough to ask us to write this book in the first place). Richard Baggaley, Jon Wainwright and Sam Clark helped us navigate the unfamiliar world of publishing without too many missteps. Francis Maude was generous enough to find the time to write us a foreword.

There are many, many people who deserve more credit for their hard work that contributed to the stories and advice collected in this book. To everyone working to make governments fit for the digital era all over the world – and especially those who worked alongside us in the GDS and other parts of the UK government – thank you. We must give similar thanks to those whose achievements on the outside gave the GDS the space to deliver what it did, like Jen Pahlka and Tom Steinberg. And for those who are still working hard on the inside, please keep going.

Most importantly, thank you to our families, and especially Hannah for her love, support and boundless patience.

About the authors

All four authors are Partners in Public Digital Ltd. Public Digital helps large international organisations, governments and senior leaders to deliver digital transformation at scale.

We have partnered with organisations in more than 20 countries, and worked in collaboration with several multilateral organisations, including the European Union and the Inter-American Development Bank.

Andrew Greenway worked in five government departments, including the Government Digital Service, where he led the team that delivered the UK's digital service standard. He also led a government review into applications of the Internet of Things, commissioned from Government's Chief Scientific Advisor by the UK Prime Minister in 2014. He now writes for several UK and international publications on government and institutional reform.

Ben Terrett was Director of Design at the Government Digital Service, where he led the multidisciplinary design team for GOV.UK which won the Design of the Year award in 2013. Before working in government, Ben was Design Director at Wieden + Kennedy and co-founder of The Newspaper Club. He is a Governor of the University of the Arts London, a member of the HS2 Design Panel and an advisor to the London Design Festival. He was inducted into the Design Week Hall of Fame in 2017.

Mike Bracken was appointed Executive Director of Digital for the UK government in 2011 and the Chief Data Officer in 2014. He was responsible for overseeing and improving the government's digital delivery of public services. After government, he sat on the board of the Co-operative Group as Chief Digital Officer. Before joining the civil service, Mike ran transformations in a variety of sectors in more than a dozen countries, including as Digital Development Director at Guardian News & Media. He was named UK Chief Digital Officer of the year in 2014 and awarded a CBE.

Tom Loosemore wrote the UK's Government Digital Strategy, and served as the GDS's deputy director for five years. He led the early development of GOV.UK. Outside government, Tom has also worked as the Director of Digital Strategy at the Co-operative Group, as a senior digital advisor to OFCOM, and was responsible for the BBC's internet strategy between 2001 and 2007.

Endnotes

1. https://www.nao.org.uk/wp-content/uploads/2015/12/E-borders-and -successor-programmes.pdf

2. Cabinet Office, Common Assessment Framework CAF 9, September 2010, version 1.4

3. https://medium.com/doteveryone/what-a-digital-organisation-looks -like-82426a210ab8

4. https://www.theatlantic.com/technology/archive/2012/11/when-the -nerds-go-marching-in/265325/

5. National Audit Office, Information and Communications Technology in government: Landscape review, para 2.8.

6. https://publications.parliament.uk/pa/cm201012/cmselect/ cmpubadm/715/71507.htm#n48

7. https://publicadministration.un.org/egovkb/en-us/Reports/ UN-E-Government-Survey-2008

8. Quarterly National Accounts – National accounts aggregates, Office for National Statistics. 2013.

9. International Monetary Fund World Economic Outlook (April 2017)

10. http://www.gao.gov/products/GAO-15-675T

11. https://www.gartner.com/newsroom/id/3368517

12. https://www.GOV.UK/government/news/digital-marketplace -transforming-how-small-businesses-sell-services-to-government

13. http://kk.org/thetechnium/the-shirky-prin/

14. https://www.huffingtonpost.com/jonha-revesencio/philippines-a -digital-lif_1_b_7199924.html

15. http://surveillance.rsf.org/en/china/

16. The full blog post is published here: https://gds.blog.GOV.UK/2013/ 03/12/were-not-appy-not-appy-at-all/

17. https://en.wikipedia.org/wiki/Digital_transformation

18. https://www.forbes.com/sites/johnkotter/2011/09/15/can-i-use-this -method-for-change-in-my-organisation/#2d1c6cdb1ce6

19. https://gilest.org/normal-words.html
20. http://www.abc.net.au/news/2016-09-01/canada-ibm-payroll
    -debacle-echoes-queensland-health/7802944
21. https://www.theguardian.com/australia-news/2017/jan/09/
    ombudsman-launches-investigation-into-centrelink-debt
    -recovery-crisis
22. https://www.computerworlduk.com/it-vendors/universal-credit
    -it-write-offs-will-reach-500m-claims-hodge-3582955/
23. http://www.bbc.co.uk/news/technology-40297493
24. http://www.telegraph.co.uk/news/2017/05/27/british-airways-chaos
    -computer-systems-crash-across-world-causing/
25. http://www.independent.co.uk/life-style/gadgets-and-tech/news/
    data-leak-swedish-government-prime-minister-stefan-lofven
    -election-latest-a7863186.html
26. http://mashable.com/2012/01/20/kodak-digital-missteps/
    #FzkG3Csj.qqt
27. Ibid.
28. https://arxiv.org/ftp/arxiv/papers/1409/1409.0003.pdf
29. https://www.instituteforgovernment.org.uk/explainers/
    big-vs-small-infrastructure-projects-does-size-matter
30. http://fortune.com/2017/09/13/ford-ceo-jim-hackett-interview/
31. https://www.theguardian.com/politics/2016/sep/05/nick-clegg
    -michael-gove-lib-dem-coalition-idealogue
32. The full text of the letter is here: https://www.GOV.UK/government/
    publications/directgov-2010-and-beyond-revolution-not-evolution
    -a-report-by-martha-lane-fox
33. https://youtu.be/OIlxdpfu71o
34. An episode labelled 'the worst failure in the history of public
    administration in Australia', where a $6 million contract led to a $1.2
    billion bill and 80,000 medical staff being paid incorrectly.
35. https://gds.blog.GOV.UK/2011/09/19/introducing-the-needotron
    -working-out-the-shape-of-the-product/
36. http://mikebracken.com/blog/on-policy-and-delivery/; Institute for
    Government, October 2014.
37. http://www.britishroadsignproject.co.uk/jock-kinneir
    -margaret-calvert/
38. Leisa Reichelt, http://www.disambiguity.com/alphagov/

39. http://www.literacytrust.org.uk/adult_literacy/illiterate_adults _in_england

40. http://contentdesign.london/home/book/

41. https://gds.blog.GOV.UK/2015/07/10/you-cant-be-half-agile/

42. Or any other stationery shop.

43. This blog post from Hillary Hartley, the Chief Digital Office of Ontario, is a great example: https://medium.com/ontariodigital/ hello-ontario-f11c4e0a847

44. https://blog.mattedgar.com/2015/05/12/most-of-government-is -mostly-service-design-most-of-the-time-discuss/

45. Reg Ward and Ted Doggett. 1991. *Keeping Score: The First Fifty Years of the Central Statistical Office.* Central Statistical Office.

46. A very helpful place to start is: http://www.wardleymaps.com/

47. Pagers are still relatively common devices in parts of the NHS (the organisation uses 10% of the world's remaining supply), with 130,000 nestling in pockets alongside nurses' personal smartphones. https:// www.theguardian.com/society/2017/sep/09/old-technology -nhs-uses-10-of-worlds-pagers-at-annual-cost-of-66m

48. http://www.bbc.co.uk/news/entertainment-arts-22164715

49. This is how a 'digital strategy' is broadly defined by GCHQ (of all places), in their excellent paper Boiling Frogs. It is available on Github at https://github.com/gchq/BoilingFrogs

50. https://designnotes.blog.GOV.UK/2015/06/22/good-services -are-verbs-2/

51. https://www.mckinsey.com/industries/public-sector/our-insights/ deliverology-from-idea-to-implementation

52. https://www.GOV.UK/government/publications/digital-efficiency- report. The GDS ultimately saved the government £4.1 billion between 2011-15, through a combination of digital and IT savings.

53. http://www.civilserviceworld.com/articles/news/whitehall -dependent-supersized-outsourcing-contracts-says -taxpayers%E2%80%99-alliance